**Arts and ethnography in a contemporary world: From learning to social participation**

## the Tufnell Press,

London,
United Kingdom
www.tufnellpress.co.uk
email contact@tufnellpress.co.uk

**British Library Cataloguing-in-Publication Data**
A catalogue record for this book is
available from the British Library

| | |
|---|---|
| *paperback ISBN* | *1872767796* |
| *ISBN-13* | *978-1-872767-79-6* |
| *Kindle* | *978-1-872767-84-0* |

Cover based on a design by Andreia Lima

# Arts and ethnography in a contemporary world: From learning to social participation

edited by
**Lígia Ferro and David Poveda**

The Ethnography and Education book series aims to publish a range of authored and edited collections including both substantive research projects and methodological texts and in particular we hope to include recent PhDs. Our priority is for ethnographies that prioritise the experiences and perspectives of those involved and that also reflect a sociological perspective with international significance. We are particularly interested in those ethnographies that explicate and challenge the effects of educational policies and practices and interrogate and develop theories about educational structures, policies and experiences. We value ethnographic methodology that involves long-term engagement with those studied in order to understand their cultures, that use multiple methods of generating data and that recognise the centrality of the researcher in the research process.

www.ethnographyandeducation.org

The editors welcome substantive proposals that seek to:

> explicate and challenge the effects of educational policies and practices and
> interrogate and develop theories about educational structures, policies and experiences,
> highlight the agency of educational actors,
> provide accounts of how the everyday practices of those engaged in education and instrumental in social reproduction.

The editors are
Professor Dennis Beach, University College of Borås, Sweden,
Professor Sofia Marques da Silva, Porto University, Portuagal,
Professor Geoff Troman, Roehampton University, London and
Professor Geoffrey Walford, University of Oxford.

Details of recent titles in this series can be found at the end of this book

# Contents

## Acknowledgments

We would like to thank to Bob Jeffrey and Dennis Beach for challenging us to organise the ETHNOARTS Conference from where this publication came out. Our thanks are extended to the colleagues from the ETHNOARTS Organising Committee: João Teixeira Lopes, Pat Thomson, Natália Azevedo, Irene Serafino, Ana Veloso, Gil Fesch and Rute Teixeira. Also we would like to express our great appreciation to Carl Bagley for providing a starting point for the ETHNOARTS conference discussions by delivering a stimulating keynote speech. Last but not the least, our special thanks to all the colleagues who participated in this conference, making comments and suggestions to the papers published in this book.

# Contributors

Giovanna Bacchiddu is a social anthropologist trained in the UK (LSE and St Andrews University), currently working as a lecturer at the Pontificia Universidad Católica de Chile in Santiago de Chile. Her work has focussed on aspects of kinship, religion and sociality in a small island of Chiloé, southern Chile, where she has been doing ethnographic research for nearly two decades. She has also conducted research on a case of international adoption, and on formal versus informal learning in young children. She has authored several articles on her research themes.

Dennis Beach is currently Professor of Education at the Department of Education and Special Education at the University of Gothenburg, and the Academy of Library, Information and Educational Science and IT at the University of Borås. He is a past chief editor for journal *Ethnography and Education*, and a senior editor for the *Oxford Encyclopedia of Education Research*. He is also the co-editor (alongside Sofia Marques da Silva and Carl Bagley) of *The Wiley Handbook of Ethnography of Education* (2018). His research interests lie within ethnography and the sociology and politics of education and teacher education. He has published extensively in these fields, in research journals and book chapters and he has also authored, co-authored and edited internationally published books in relation to education policy, education and equity, education and marginalisation, and the politics of education and teacher education reform. He is particularly interested in the intersections between social class and race in the politics, policies and history of education inclusion and exclusion in the Nordic Countries.

Geoff Bright is a research fellow in the Education and Social Research Institute at Manchester Metropolitan University (UK). He trained in philosophy and his PhD was an ethnography of class, place and gender as it impacts on education in UK coal-mining communities. He has recently completed four AHRC Connected Communities projects which use arts-based methods and the idea of a 'social haunting' to re-imagine futures for such communities (see www.socialhaunting.com). He also involved in politicised sonic practice as an improvising musician and experimental vocalist.

Lígia Ferro is assistant professor and a researcher at the Institute of Sociology and the Sociology Department, Universidade do Porto (Portugal). Ferro was a visiting scholar at universities in Europe, the United States of America and Brazil. She is the author, co-author and editor of several publications, including the books *Arts and Cultural Education in a World of Diversity* (2019, Springer) and *Moving Cities: Contested Views on Urban Life* (2018, Springer). Lately she has been working on urban street cultures, arts education, migrations and action research especially applying ethnographic methods. Currently Ferro is a member of the Executive Committee of the European Sociological Association (ESA), vocal of the Directive Committee of the Portuguese Sociological Association and member of the board of the European Network of Observatories in the Field of Arts and Cultural Education (ENO).

Anton Franks is a Research Associate at the School of Education, University of Nottingham, currently researching community-based arts projects attached to the Serpentine Galleries in London. A teacher of drama and English in inner London schools, he was then a teacher educator and researcher at the Institute of Education, London and Associate Professor in the area of creativity, arts and education at the University of Nottingham and the University of Warwick. Recent publications include *Teachers, arts practice and pedagogy* in Changing English, *Drama and the representation of affect…* in Research in Drama Education, and *Drama and Learning* in the Oxford Research Encyclopedia of Education.

Andrew Hewitt is Associate Professor in Fine Art: Art & the Public Sphere, at the University of Northampton. He is a practising artist, writer and educator in the Partisan Social Club. His PhD was entitled *Art and Counter Publics in Third Way Cultural Policy*. Hewitt was a member of the Freee art collective from 2004-2018. His work has been exhibited at Milton Keynes Gallery, the Istanbul Biennial and the Liverpool Biennial as well as BAK, Utrecht, Wysing Arts, Cambridge and SMART Project Space, Amsterdam, ICA, London. He is a founding editor of *Art and the Public Sphere* Journal.

Anton Hunter is a PhD candidate in music composition at Manchester Metropolitan University. Active in the field of free improvisation and contemporary jazz, Anton performs regularly around the UK and Europe, and has been running jazz and improvised music events in Manchester for around fifteen years. His doctoral research is a practice-as-research enquiry into composing for large groups of improvising musicians. More information: www.antonhunter.com

Mel Jordan is Head of Contemporary Art at the Royal College of Art, London (UK). She is a artist, writer and educator in the Partisan Social Club. Jordan was a member of the Freee art collective from 2004-2018. Her work has been exhibited at Milton Keynes Gallery, the Istanbul Biennial, the Liverpool Biennial as well as BAK, Utrecht, Wysing Arts, Cambridge and SMART Project Space, Amsterdam, ICA, London. Her PhD was entitled *Art, its function and its publics: Public sphere theory in the work of the Freee art collective 2004-2012*. She is a principle editor of *Art & the Public Sphere*, Intellect Ltd., ISSN 2042-793X. View recent research activity here: researchonline.rca.ac.uk/view/creators/Jordan=3AMel=3A=3A.html

Amy McKelvie is Curator for Schools and Teachers programmes across Tate Modern and Tate Britain. She is interested in the role of affect in art and learning, as part of her MA in Contemporary Art Theory at Goldsmith she has looked at the productivity of embarrassment as a response to performance art.

David Poveda is an associate professor at the Universidad Autónoma de Madrid (Spain). He has training in Psychology, Education, Social Anthropology and extensive experience in sociolinguistic/linguistic ethnographic research. His research interests include children's linguistic and semiotic practices and the interconnections between social diversity, education, development and social inequality. More information: www.uam.es/david.poveda

Otávio Raposo is an Invited Assistant Professor at the University Institute of Lisbon (ISCTE-IUL) and postdoctoral researcher in Anthropology at the Centre for Research and Studies in Sociology (CIES-IUL). He has participated in several research projects about urban studies, youth cultures, segregation, art and migrations in Portugal and Brazil. He is currently addressing artistic practices and the civic engagement of young people from the outskirts of Lisbon, as well as the public politics addressed to them. He has made some documentaries, including *Nu Bai. Lisbon's Black Rap* and *ImigraSom*.

Harriet Rowley is a lecturer in Education and Community at Manchester Metropolitan University (MMU). Her first degree is in Philosophy, she is a qualified secondary school teacher and was awarded her PhD from The University of Manchester in 2013. She is an experienced ethnographic researcher predominantly working in education, social care and community-based settings. She has co-produced arts-based projects with young people and adults leading precarious lives both in the UK and internationally.

Francisco Schwember is an artist, professor and curator. He has a Fine Arts degree (2001), an Art Teacher Training (2002), Master in Fine Arts (2010), PhD in Education, from the Pontificia Universidad Católica de Chile. He has participated in more than sixty exhibitions, both in Chile and abroad (New York, Madrid, Buenos Aires, Lima, Havana, Cape Town, Quito, Berlin). In addition to developing a research and creation proposal linked to Arts-Based Research and Interdiscipline, he has worked as a Professor in Fine Arts since 2002 at the Fine Arts School of Catholic University of Chile, teaching in various courses, both in the areas of Painting and in Workshops of Creation. He is also a professor of the Master's program in Cultural Heritage of the School of Architecture. His work focuses on the relationship between art, education and first nations, based on a transdisciplinary approach that addresses action research as a collective work methodology.

Ricardo Seiça Salgado is an anthropologist and a performer, integrated research member at CRIA – Centre for Research in Anthropology (Portugal, University of Minho). He develops a research project in between ethnographic and artistic research methodologies, particularly ethnotheatre as research action and radical pedagogy. He has training on performance studies, focusing on the behaviour of alternative resistance in contexts of marginality, and the mechanics of dramatic play as a way of producing worlds of being. As performer, he recently develops independent solo performances. He is curator and cofounder of *baldio* — performance studies, an independent Portuguese research group.

Pat Thomson is Convenor of the Centre for Research in Arts, Creativity and Literacy (CRACL), University of Nottingham. She is known for her interdisciplinary engagement with questions of creative and socially just learning and change. Much of this work has been in collaboration with Professor Christine Hall. Pat has had a long term research partnership with Professor Barbara Kamler with whom she writes about academic writing. She is an Editor of the international peer refereschoolsed journal, *Educational Action Research* (Taylor and Francis). Her current research focuses on creativity, the arts and change in schools and communities, and postgraduate writing pedagogies. She has expertise in policy, sociology and cultural geography and has a particular interest in text-based and arts informed research methods. She frequently uses visual research methods in her work.

Leanne Turvey began curating Schools and Teachers programmes at Tate Modern in 2008, becoming Convenor for Schools and Teachers programmes at Tate Modern and Tate Britain in a collaborative job share with Alice Walton in 2010. In this role they head a large cross-site team, developing artist-led programming for teachers and students. Leanne has previously worked as Education Coordinator for Camden Arts Centre and Chisenhale Gallery, as Youth Arts Programmer for Look Ahead Housing and Care and as an art teacher in Camden schools. In 2017 she worked as part of the Faculty for *aneducation, Documenta 14*.

Begoña Vigo Arrazola is a senior lecturer at the Faculty of Education in the University of Saragosse (Spain) and she is a member of the consolidated research team *Education and Diversity (EDI)*. Much of her work has been conducted in relation to these issues including coordination, participation and supervision of different national and international projects. The analysis of inclusive educational processes and practices in rural and urban spaces and its conceptualisation in educational policy combined with critical ethnography have been published in different journal articles and book chapters.

Alice Walton started working within the Learning department at Tate Modern as the Teachers Curator in 2007, becoming Convenor for Schools and Teachers programmes at Tate Modern and Tate Britain in a collaborative job share with Leanne Turvey in 2010. In this role they head a large cross-site team responsible for developing artist-led programming for teachers and students. In her capacity as a practising artist, Alice has worked with numerous galleries and organisations to implement learning programmes designed to support teacher and student engagement with contemporary artists.

# Arts and ethnography in a contemporary world: An introduction

*Lígia Ferro and David Poveda*

## 1. Presentation

The story behind this book begins in the 2015 Oxford Ethnography and Education Conference. Several of the presentations there and more or less informal discussions, in and outside the conference sessions, pointed to an interest in and a need to discuss and put into dialogue different perspectives on the role of ethnography when approaching arts practices and learning. A first step, taken alongside Pat Thomson (University of Nottingham), was a proposal for a special issue of the Journal *Ethnography and Education* entitled *Ethnographic Explorations of the Arts and Education*. The response to the Call for Papers for the special issue was overwhelming with more than thirty very interesting proposals (many more than can fit in a journal special issue) that culminated with the publication of the special issue in 2018 (Poveda, Thomson and Ferro, 2018). The reaction suggested that generating a discussion space in the field by organising a scientific meeting, in which the colleagues participating in this publication and others interested in the discussion could meet, would be well received.

Thus, we decided to organise this meeting at the Faculdade de Letras, Universidade do Porto, Portugal from 21st to 23rd of June, 2017. The *ETHNOARTS — Ethnographic Explorations of the Arts and the Education Conference*[1] received seventy proposals for oral communication, fifty-five of

1. For more details please see www.facebook.com/ethnoartsporto/ Institutions involved in the organisation: Instituto de Sociologia, Universidade do Porto, IS-UP; Departamento de Sociologia, Universidade do Porto, DS-UP; Centre for Research in Arts, Creativity and Literacies, Nottingham University; Facultad de Psicología, Universidad Autónoma de Madrid, UAM; Ethnography and Education, E & E; Centro de Investigação e Estudos em Sociologia, CIES-IUL, ISCTE-IUL; Centro de Investigação em Psicologia da Música e Educação Musical, CIPEM, INET, IPP; Centro de Estudos de Sociologia e Estética Musical, CESEM, FCSH-UNL. The organising committee was composed by Lígia Ferro, João Teixeira Lopes, Pat Thomson, David Poveda, Natália Azevedo, Irene Serafino, Ana Veloso, Gil Fesch and Rute Teixeira. The keynote speech was delivered by Carl Bagley, to whom we would like to thank for providing an extraordinarily stimulating starting point for the conference discussions. Funding: Fundação para a Ciência e a Tecnologia, Reitoria

which were selected for presentation in a small-scale conference aimed at fostering as much discussion as possible. The meeting included PhD students, post-doctoral researchers, university faculty and artists from twelve countries. Feedback from the event was very positive and colleagues in the final session suggested organising a publication drawing from a selection of the papers presented at the meeting.

This edited volume draws from contributions to the ETHNOARTS conference and captures the growing international attention to research developing at the juncture of various disciplinary concerns. On the one hand, educational ethnographic research has turned its attention to learning, teaching and educational practices around art across a variety of institutional and community settings. On the other hand, artists and art researchers have turned to the methodological toolkit of ethnography as a more productive approach to their research aims. In this field, ethnography interconnects to various disciplines beyond Anthropology and showcases its dynamic and multi-faced nature but also several of the tensions and uncertainties that emerge as researchers experiment with ethnographic approaches and extend conventional research practices. Artistic practices and art settings in the contemporary world are also a social field in which definitional issues around learning, education, social participation, expressive practices or the various manifestations of art are constantly re-examined.

Ethnography is a methodology historically linked with Anthropology but nowadays is used by a diversity of academics and professionals. The use of ethnography in a wide range of disciplines and contexts makes it a dynamic and challenging method. Studies on and in the arts often blur conventional disciplinary borders, allowing for new insights to arise from interdisciplinary dialogues. By combining the study of social practices and discourses related to art-making, and by applying ethnography as the main methodological approach, researchers bypass frontiers, a condition for a stimulating intellectual debate. The nine chapters in this book capture this diversity of issues by presenting detailed ethnographic studies of artistic practices, art contexts or artistic interventions in settings across locations in Europe and Latin America. The book includes texts written by colleagues working in the United Kingdom, Portugal, Spain, Sweden and Chile. All chapters are firmly grounded on ethnographic research

da Universidade do Porto and Instituto de Sociologia da Universidade do Porto. The book of abstracts is published and available online: repositorio-aberto.up.pt/bitstream/10216/105895/2/202484.pdf and present a balance of methodological discussions around ethnographic methods stemming from the examination of artistic practices and settings, detailed accounts of how art is experienced in local settings or critical accounts of how art emerges as a methodological and conceptual tool for social intervention, promoting social participation and educational change.

As we see it, the book is structured in two parts. The first one focuses on arts, ethnography and learning in different settings and comprises the first four chapters. These texts focus on how learning through the arts practice can impact a diverse group of protagonists of art projects in museums and galleries and in schools, taking into consideration, with more or less emphasis in each of the chapters, the interconnections with the wider community in which the projects are implemented. The interactions between professionals with several disciplinary backgrounds are taken seriously by all of the authors, who try to analyse how different professional knowledges (cf., Mercado, 2002) and experiences have implications for practice in such kind of projects. The second part of the book includes the following five chapters. Here ethnography and arts practices turn to the examination of the methodological process and its implications for data collection and the analysis of results. The concept of participation is, with more or less emphasis, at the center of the five contributions. At least two cross-cutting questions emerge across chapters: How can arts practice promote or constrain social participation? How can ethnography help (if it can) deepen our understanding of the processes involved in artistic practice and learning?

## 2. Outline of the contributions

The first chapter of the book, authored by Thomson, McKelvie, Turvey and Walton, is an experimental text consisting of a dialogue between the Tate Modern teachers—McKelvie, Turvey and Walton—and the anthropologist/researcher—Pat Thomson. Starting from the notion that ethnographers are engaged in *co-constructed research* (e.g. Holland, Renold, Ross and Hillman, 2010; Spindler and Hammond, 2006) and in 'research which takes up new materialist and/or queer positionalities' (e.g. Aarsand and Forsberg, 2010; Fenwick, Doyle, Michael and Scoles, 2015; Hickey-Moody, 2012; Maclure, Holmes, MacRae and Jones, 2010), the authors reflect on rich description, text, writing and representation. They consider writing as an important part of the ethnographic method, but also as thinking and, thus, a way of producing reality. Writing is seen as 'doing work in the world, rather than as an object to be categorised and codified'. The authors have been working together for six years and the dialogue established in this text reflects the results of the regular joint work revealing interesting insights of the interdisciplinary dialogues established between them. The Lexicon is a long text co-written by the authors starting from their experience at the Tate Summer Schools, where they developed a *shared language* to talk about understanding of gallery pedagogies. The authors recur to the Lexicon to go deeper in the analysis. Writing is then seen as emergence, in the logics of an experimental ethnography, and art is seen as a happening 'in between the viewer and the work'. This chapter is an effort to go further beyond the work condensed in the Lexicon.

Chapter two by Franks brings to the debate the potential of an arts education project carried out at the Serpentine Gallery in London, for individual, social and cultural change in the city. The reflections on learning try to focus on the perspectives and experiences of all the project participants (children, artist, curators, researcher and staff of the Portman Early Childhood Centre). Also by developing a rich ethnography, the author tries to grasp 'patterns of playful activity in developing emergent aspects of personhood'. Starting from the definition of culture drawn by Williams (1992), the researcher analyses the ways in which the developed project 'acknowledges and facilitates' children's 'sense of agency' and 'offers resources' in the 'free-wheeling creativity of their play with materials and the narratives that they construct'. Learning through 'stuff' that 'makes people as much as people make stuff' (Miller, 2010) reveals certain patterns of activity in which interferes the ways how adults assist the children's play. Franks' work shows clearly how classifications are built by adults and are questioned through children's play, what becomes (or should become) a central part of the learning process.

Vigo and Beach, in the third chapter, build from the work developed by Beach and Dovemark (2007) in which creative teaching practices are seen as a part of material reality and set out to contribute to understanding the 'sense of art connected with an education for all' and the 'complexity of lived educational situations'. The school where the research was completed is located in a peri-urban small town in Aragón (Spain) and works according to a 'creative teaching perspective' (Vigo and Soriano, 2014), which gives emphasis to the mediations between the learning process in the classroom and the events outside this space. The researchers worked in a quite challenging environment in terms of educational circumstances, especially because the children's parents are migrant unskilled agricultural workers with very different cultural backgrounds. Vigo and Beach use an ethnographic research method to 'identify, describe, explain and define teaching practices' and children's involvement in learning, where art is used in different subjects in the school curriculum. More than a way of expression, here art is a 'tool of mediation' because it served to 'overcome social distance and linguistic difficulties/complications', particularly when the creation of 'personally meaningful learning experiences' takes place. Following Freire's (1972/2000) thoughts on art, the authors found out that art practices allowed giving space to children's culture and supported their emerging subjectivity and school based formal and informal learning. The authors suggest that education through the arts should be considered in the formal curriculum in order to 'enable more positive social relations between teacher and pupils'.

The fourth chapter presents Bacchiddu and Schwember's analysis focused on the process and results of a multidisciplinary project led by an anthropologist and an artist in a rural school, located in an indigenous area of southern of Chile, the island of Apiao. The text builds from both perspectives, that one of the anthropologist and the one by the artist, trying to reach a common point of understanding of the project process and results. In particular, they note that the children are very independent at home but that dependency on the teachers' instructions is promoted at school. Also, they realised that students are interested in activities resembling their regular home activities and that there are obstacles to recover 'traditional aspects of knowledge' like local cultural traits. The authors underscore that the focus of the national school curriculum on 'national requirements' treats the schools as if they were part of an homogeneous universe, ignoring cultural and geographic specificities. By implementing the project *Territorios Alternos*, the authors could 'integrate knowledge originated and managed by the community itself' and, simultaneously, involve the community as an active part of the creative and research process, using arts as a fundamental tool. By discussing contrasts between children's behaviour inside and outside school, this chapter highlights the interconnections between learning and social participation and can also be seen at the intersection of the two major themes we have identified as organisers of the volume.

The second part of the book includes five chapters where arts are also analysed from an ethnographic perspective but in which the concepts of social and, sometimes political, participation arise more clearly as food for thought. In chapter five Hewitt and Jordan take Hal Foster's essay *Artist as Ethnographer* (1995) as a starting point to examine some recent UK research projects in which artists and sociologists have collaborated. The variety of ways of interdisciplinary collaboration frequently fail to acknowledge the 'critical function of art and its relationship to politics'. By analysing a collaborative project by the *Freee* art collective and the Forum for Democratic Practices, the authors conclude that it is crucial to understand the 'antagonistic aspect of each field' to attain a successful interdisciplinary collaboration. Ethnography, arts practice and participation are key concepts of Hewitt and Jordan's chapter to understand some fundamental misrecognitions and their contribution will certainly help to overcome them.

Chapter six titled *Ethnotheatre: expanding participant observation* by Salgado brings the reader to research using ethno-theatre, an art-based methodology built from ethnography and theatre. By dramatising personal, cultural and social perspectives of real life, the author argues that this tool expands the possibilities of fieldwork. Salgado proposes a kit to apply the ethno-theatre methodology taking into account many aspects such as the researcher's entrance and roles in the field, involving a more collaborative posture, a new perspective of the ethnographic interview and the processes by which ethnographic fieldnotes and other registers are replicated in the texts and performances and pour into different modes of expression. In order to explore this methodological tool, the author discusses data from two ethno-theatre research projects: one carried out inside a Portuguese prison and other developed within the city of *Coimbra's Academy Theatrical Initiation Circle* (CITAC) project.

In chapter seven Bright and Hunter start from the concept of 'social aesthetics' of improvisation (Born, Lewis and Straw, 2017) to analyse the performance culture of a Manchester collective called *The Manchester Improv Collective*. Art performance practices, including the musical expression, are 'immanently social' and can, in improvised arrangements, *empractice* 'novel realms of social experience, new modes of sociality' (Born, Lewis and Straw, 2017: 9). By analysing the participation of social actors who are mostly under thirty years-old, Bright and Hunter discuss how *empractice* shows up in the settings of diverse playing formats at *The Manchester Improv Collective*. This framework corresponds to a renewed interest in the articulations between politics, aesthetics and ethics in arts-based practice. Ethnographic methodological boundaries are shifted, following the challenge proposed by Bagley (2009), as the authors think about how well are we, as ethnographers, equipped to collect and analyse 'the sensuous array of sights, sounds, and smells as well as represent the traumas, passions and emotions, of twenty-first century lived experiences'. The authors draw upon Pink's (2009) *sensory ethnography* and Stewart's (2007) approach to the contingent *worlding* of *ordinary affects* to answer some of these challenges.

In *Lost and found: Ethnographic researcher and arts practitioners getting lost and coming home* (chapter eight) Rowley leads us to think about participation and representation related with democratic practice by discussing the results of an ethnographic study carried out at an arts and social care charity for homeless men in Manchester, United Kingdom. The broader frame of the research is an *EU Horizon 2020* project, PARTISPACE, where spaces and styles of youth participation across eight European cities are analysed. The particular case here highlighted by Rowley, consisted of a series of installations formed as planters with light boxes, including walking tours to the sights where these installations were placed and a film documentary. The author seeks to find the communicative possibilities of art practices when used in articulation with ethnographic techniques 'to explore what is made visible or heard, which might not have otherwise been possible'.

Last, but not the least, in chapter nine Raposo presents research carried out at Quinta do Mocho, in the city of Loures, part of the metropolitan area of Lisbon, Portugal, where an urban art project was implemented. Starting from an originally illegal and subversive practice, graffiti, the author mentions how it is being legitimised in the art field, but more than that, Raposo shows how urban art is a tool for promotion by the municipality, that is trying to change the social image of Quinta do Mocho. The young residents of this suburban and poor neighbourhood were turned into community guides of this open air art gallery visited by a large number of tourists. The researcher developed an ethnography, namely by following the guided tours, seeking answers to rethink urban segregation policies, participation and the role of art in the processes.

In short, by crossing several sights of research where arts practices and ethnography are at the core of the analysis, the authors of the nine chapters make a valuable contribution to our understanding on the way ethnography can grasp the roles and reconfigurations of arts in a contemporary world. This edited book should be of interest to scholars and practitioners across a number of social and human disciplines (Sociology, Anthropology, Psychology, Education, etc.), artistic disciplines (Theatre, Music, Dance, Visual, Plastic Arts, etc.) and work settings (Schools, Academia, Museums, Associations, Community Organisations, Non-Governmental Organisations, etc.) interested in methodological questions and substantive research emerging at the intersection of ethnography, art, learning and participation in a changing world.

# References

Aarsand, P. and Forsberg, L., (2010) Producing children's corporeal privacy: ethnographic video recording as material discursive practice, *Qualitative Research,* 10(2):249-268.

Bagley, C., (2009) Guest editorial: Shifting boundaries in ethnographic methodology, *Ethnography and Education,* 4(3):251-254.

Beach, D. and Dovemark, M., (2007) *Education and the commodity problem: Ethnographic investigations of creativity and performativity in Swedish schools,* London: the Tufnell Press.

Born, G., Lewis, E. and Straw, W., (2017) *Improvisation and social aesthetics,* Durham, North Carolina: Duke University Press.

Fenwick, T., Doyle, S., Michael, M., and Scoles, J., (2015) Matters of learning and education: Sociomaterial approaches in ethnographic research, in Boling, S., Honing, M-S., Neumann, S. and Seele, C., (eds.) *MultiPluriTrans in educational ethnography: Approaching the multimodality, plurality and translocality of educational realities.* Bielefeld: Transcript Verlag/Columbia University Press.

Foster, H.,(1995) *The Artist as Ethnographer?,* in Marcus, G. and Myers, F., (eds.) *Refiguring Art and Anthropology,* Berkeley: University of California Press.

Freire, P., (1972/2000) *Pedagogy of the oppressed* (30th anniversary ed.), New York: Continuum.

Hickey-Moody, A., (2012) *Youth, arts and education: Reassembling subjectivity through affect,* London: Routledge.

Holland, S., Renold, E., Ross, N. J. and Hillman, A., (2010) Power, agency and participatory agendas: A critical exploration of young people's engagement in participative qualitative research. *Childhood,* 17(3):360-375.

Maclure, M., Holmes, R., MacRae, C. and Jones, L. (2010) Animating classroom ethnography: overcoming video fear. *International Journal of Qualitative Studies in Education,* 23(5):543-556.

Mercado, R., (2002), *Los saberes docentes como construcción social [Teaching knowledges as social construction],* México DF: Fondo de Cultura Económica.

Miller, D., (2010) *Stuff,* Cambridge, Polity.

Pink, S., (2009) *Doing sensory ethnography,* London: Sage.

Poveda, D; Thomson, P. and Ferro, L., (2018), Ethnographic explorations of the arts and education: an introduction, *Ethnography and Education,* 13(3):269-272.

Spindler, G. and Hammond, L. (eds.), (2006) *Innovations in educational ethnography: Theory, methods, and results,* New York: Psychology Press.

Stewart, K., (2007) *Ordinary affects,* Durham, NC: Duke University Press.

Vigo, B., and Soriano, J., (2014) Teaching practices and teachers' perceptions of group creative practices in inclusive rural schools, *Ethnography and Education,* 9(3):253-269.

Williams, R., (1992) *The long revolution,* London, The Hogarth Press.

Chapter 1

# Learning the art museum: Experiments in talking/writing ethnography

*Pat Thomson, Amy McKelvie, Leanne Turvey and Alice Walton*

We are interested not so much in what ethnographic writing *is*, but rather, what it *does*                                          (after Deleuze, 1995, p. 21).

This is a perhaps an experimental ethnographic text. Maybe this contention is explained as the writing proceeds. We can say to begin with that it is a deliberate action, we have worked to create a text that mirrors our experience of working with art and each other. We offer a bricolage of insights inter-mingled with ethnographic data, a constellation of points of view. Rather than impose a narrative which creates the illusion that we have a coherent and unified position, we have instead curated topics that invite readers to make their own connections. As it happens, this text is rather like our regular shared conversations.

## 1. Anthropologists have been engaged in debates about writing for a long time

Anthropologists have long been concerned with writing. Arguably anthropology is *the* discipline, outside of English and language and linguistics, that has been most concerned with the ways in which scholarly writing produces particular kinds of knowledge. The *linguistic turn*—understanding language as a social construction, as specific, particular and situated—spoke to the dilemmas of engaging with cultures other than one's own. Anthropologists worried about the un-translatability of concepts and terminology, the potential for misunderstanding and more significantly, misappropriation of indigenous knowledges, and the colonialist origins and potential imperialist consequences of their projects. They worried about their writing and themselves as authors (Geertz, 1988).

Still and moving images and *rich description* were used in efforts to provide more accurate *impartial* modes of anthropological observation and modes of communication. But, at the same time, anthropologists also recognised that what they offered by way of written field notes and final reports could not be impartial—it was unavoidably mediated through their own subjectivity/ ies. No matter how reflexive, how thorough their coding and thematising, anthropological researchers were always implicated in their accounts (Clifford and Marcus, 1986; Rosaldo, 1989). And participants had agency; they might in fact be highly offended or completely bemused by anthropological interpretations of their cultures (Brettell, 1996). This realisation perhaps accounts for the near ubiquity of the concept *representation* in anthropological writing about writing—writing is not mimesis and accounts are always best approximations (Noblit, Flores, and Murillo, 2004).

In recent years, anthropologists have continued to address concerns about disciplinary knowledge-making practices and the ways in which writing is implicated in them. Who is counted as the writer and how they are to be textually presented has shifted—ethnographers write themselves into the text (Reed-Danahay, 1997; Ty and Verduyn, 2008); participatory and co-constructed research and writing is undertaken as a move counter to misogyny and colonialism (Lassiter, 2005; Visweswaren, 1994). Language and image are under duress—the practices of naming and categorisation have been de-naturalised and made highly problematic (Rabinow, 2007; Rabinow, Marcus, Faubion and Rees, 2008); sensory and affective approaches to generating, analysing and presenting research experiences and ideas are undertaken (Behar, 1996; Pink, 2009); and more creative, rhizomatic and live approaches to data generation and analysis are incorporated into anthropological practice, pedagogies and texts (Back and Puwar, 2013; Ingold, 2011). Writing itself has become an object of debate (Atkinson and Delamont, 2008; Narayan, 2012)—arts based genres are used to both generate and present research (Denzin, 1997; Ellis and Bochner, 1996); and the post-human—materials, objects and networks—decentres human practices and interactions as the primary focus of investigation leading to new forms of multi-modal texts (Fox and Alldred, 2015; Ingold, 2000).

Very little is settled within anthropology as a discipline, including the central practice of writing. According to George Marcus, we are left to imagine what new ethnographic textual practices might be, in studios, labs and design spaces, to deal with the 'movements and contexts of fieldwork—both naturalistic and contrived, collaborative and individualistic' (Marcus, 2012: 432).

## 2. While a smaller field, concerns about writing and knowledge production have been taken up in educational ethnography

These more recent debates and experiments have permeated the practices of educational ethnography. Mills and Morton (2013) for instance identify a division in educational ethnography between (1) educational ethnographers who hold to possibilities of distance and objectivity managed through processes of quasi-scientised processes of data analysis, and writing which removes the researcher from the text and (2) educational ethnographers who recognise affect, use a range of analytic approaches including arts based, and who work with and from their own subjectivity in the text. However, the landscape is perhaps more complex than Mills and Morton suggest. Educational ethnographers are engaged in co-constructed research (e.g. Holland, Renold, Ross and Hillman, 2010; Spindler and Hammond, 2006), and in research which takes up new materialist and/or queer positionalities (e.g. Aarsand and Forsberg, 2010; Fenwick, Doyle, Michael and Scoles, 2015; Hickey-Moody, 2012; Maclure, Holmes, MacRae and Jones, 2010)—these challenge notions of rich description, text, writing and representation.

The journal *Ethnography and Education* has published some of this work, for instance, papers which:

Explore the implications of information technologies. White reports on participant experiences of a video workshop (White, 2009). His text is multi-media and multi-modal—he suggests that writing about the video workshops would produce only *thin description*. However, his interest is not to produce *thick description* but rather to understand the value and impact of a specific educational experience. He argues that use of digital media affords the production of participant-produced videos—and these are open, multi-perspective *messy*, unstable texts open to viewer interpretations. Shumar and Madison (2013) offer a more challenging perspective on *the virtual*, arguing that digital technologies developed in late consumer capitalism create not simply crises in representation and in writing, but also about the ways we think about sites and field work and the ways in which we teach ethnography.

Argue for arts-based representations. VanSlyke-Briggs (2009) writes about ethno-fiction, the use of a literary genre to convey the practices, interactions and experiences recorded through conventional ethnographic research (See also Bagley, 2009). She argues that writing fiction does not mean abandoning *facts* but rather that the binary non-fiction/ fiction ignores the ways in which ethnographers are always authors/composers of texts, regardless of its final form. Ethno-fiction is a stylistic choice, rather than an onto-epistemological shift. Clough (2009) presents auto-ethnographic story-making as both research method and a representation. And there is of course a question of how such arts-based representations are to be judged—Sparkes (2009) for example proposes connoisseurship as the basis for textual evaluations.

Propose that writing can be a mode of analysis—Coles and Thomson (2016) suggest that, rather than coding and thematising, iterative writing is a systematic approach to making-meaning from field notes, connecting events and practices and integrating theoretical perspectives.

Discuss children writing ethnographically about their classroom, connecting ideas *nomadically* to construct, not *rich description*, but small stories of their everyday experiences. Hohti argues that the resulting texts are not representations but a practice which produces writing, classroom reality, children-ethnographers and research together (Hohti, 2016)—her paper however is written in a genre that is recognisably social science.

It is clear from even this minimalist survey that wider debates in anthropology about the nature of knowing, knowledge production, tools and texts have infiltrated the educational ethnographic community. However, some debates, such as the nature and status of the texts that we produce, arguably remain under-theorised and only intermittently explored. And we note, despite these contributions, the presence of some durable ethnographic reference points—field notes, and the terms rich description and representation.

### 3. Our intention and contribution

Our interest in this paper is to consider writing as both a method of research, but also as thinking. We see, as does Hohti (2016), writing texts as a way of producing reality, meanings, persons and practices. We see writing as doing work in the world, rather than as an object to be categorised and codified. We also want to hold those durable reference points up to further scrutiny.

### 4. Our 'ethnographic project'

We have been working together for six years. In addition to Pat participating in, and blogging about, annual teacher Summer Schools, we have regular full day conversations which we sometimes record. Pat's field notes and reflective memos are usually the starting point for a long exploration of a particular topic.

Sometimes we write serially, moving text around, adding and crossing out and writing over. These two sections in 4 were originally written for an internal report of a Summer School then rewritten for our shared publication, *The Lexicon*. This chapter was first authored by Pat, but rewritten and amended by the Tate team.

## The Tate Schools and Teachers team explain our partnership:

Pat was invited by Emily Pringle, Head of Learning Practice and Research, to begin a conversation with us about what teachers might learn through our Continuos Professional Development (CPD) offer. What was crucial about this conversation was Pat's openness to listen and talk with us about our practice. This conversation opened up both a pragmatic (we had sought to demonstrate to the Tate and to the wider sector the learning of teachers passing through our programme) and a vitally creative and open-ended direction. This had not been our research focus. We had developed another project where we were exploring artists' practice as a form of learning research in the museum. However, what we discovered in that first conversation was a shared ambition to find out the learning through the practice, and to generate material that we could share with the wider gallery and learning sectors.

Initially Pat took part in the Summer School 2012 as an embedded participant—drawing on her ethnographic practice. In an early planning conversation, she suggested we frame the research as 'What's going on here?' We met throughout the week-long school to discuss what she was *finding*. This first stage produced a collaborative report and introduced a way of potentially theorising the practice through a discussion of the notion of *affordances*.

After the Summer School 2012, we explored the idea of further research, this time to be constructed collaboratively with teachers and artists. This idea developed into a six-day period of co-constructing a research question involving three artists, three teachers, ourselves as Learning curators and Pat.

After the six days and a struggle to co-construct a research question, a further series of days were planned. This time the artists and teachers were to co-devise learning situations for the group to share in. It had been hoped that this would occur naturally in the first six days and that a research question would emerge. One of the tensions for this project was that we as programmers, in conversation with Pat, had begun the process of working together with a very clear overarching question: What do teachers learn through CPD at the Tate? It became clear that this submerged question, which surfaced through the different conversations held over the six days, was 'the question' and needed to be acknowledged as such.

The project shifted into the form of a reference group, involving the same group of people, established to look at the existing programme on offer to teachers. The focus for the reference group was to bring their individual expertise to the process of researching teacher learning. This shift in our plans came out of a review process where we recognised that it was important to avoid setting up a new parallel programme developed and run in a different way to how the programme itself runs. This was important mainly because we realised we needed to look at how we actually programmed if we were to test its efficacy in supporting teacher learning.

In parallel to working with us on establishing the reference group, Pat took part in the 2013, 2014, 2015, 2016, and 2017 Summer Schools. It became clear to her that each 'moment' on the programme was made very different from the last because of our practice of inviting different artists with very different practices to develop each school. Pat was instrumental in supporting us to recognise and articulate the significance of our curatorial framing of each invitation to an artist.

*Pat's account parallels this:*

I was interested in working with the Schools and Teachers (S&T) team because what they did was so dramatically different to the dominant forms of CPD on offer to teachers. S&T aimed to expose teachers to contemporary art practices. Rather than organise a pre-digested set of activities which could be simply taken back to school and *delivered*, the team saw teachers as professionals capable of working out how to convert their own learning experiences into something appropriate for their students. They made no cause and effect assumptions about what teachers might learn during the Summer Schools, although of course they hoped that they would find something in the experience both for themselves as well as for their teaching.

Like many professionals, the S&T team had had some experiences with researchers which were less than positive. The team was understandably cautious about getting involved with someone they didn't know. It was very important that we get to know each other and that we work out what each other was about. This took precedence over formulating any research project. We also did not really know what was possible and so we agreed on a very open-ended question to guide my participation in the first Summer School—what's going on here?

The research tradition I work in is ethnographic—I try to have a deep engagement over time with a group of participants. Practices of ethnography have changed over time—researchers now are more likely to work with the people in the place they are researching. Ethnographers participate in the everyday activities of the place they are interested in, and engage in ongoing conversations about what they see and think. Ethnographers also use their own experiences as part of the process of making sense of their experiences. The hallmark of ethnography is note-taking and writing. While ethnographers might make images, audio recordings, count or survey or map, the basic process is one of writing description in a field notebook. These descriptive notes are then subject to extensive analysis, often via more writing, and in dialogue with other participants (see Coles and Thomson, 2016).

As a participant in the first Summer School I paid attention to what was on offer to me, as well as to the teachers. I began by focusing on the language and activities and then on what I saw people doing and saying. I also recorded in my notebook the way that I felt at each stage of the week and I tried to check this out with other people, as unobtrusively as I could.

I developed a practice of meeting with a member of the S&T team at the beginning and end of each day and sharing the things I was thinking about. Because the team is always thinking about what they do, these times were more of a conversation than anything resembling a report. After 2012, one member from the S&T team also participated in the Summer School. Relieved of their organisational responsibilities they could focus on the kinds of experiences that were on offer. The S&T member and I then always met before and after each day. We also instituted a formal debrief. From the second Summer School this debrief also involved the artists.

Dialogue has become a key to the way in which we carry out our shared research. I often do some writing about things I've been thinking about—this is often the result of re-reading my notes, thinking and reading—and this creates a *provocation* for talking. We do a lot of talking. A lot. During the process of conversation we have been building our understandings—from the ground up and also from our reading—of key aspects of the pedagogies of the S&T team. While we had an option to simply focus first of all on what teachers get from the Summer School, we decided to consolidate our current understandings in answer to the more open question 'what's going on here?'

This covers teachers', but also our own as well as artists' learning. We might be building a theory of gallery education—or not.

There are some similarities between ethnographic and artistic practice. Both are unashamedly interpretive and work through researcher/artist subjectivity. Both rely on noticing, listening in, tuning in. Both take as long as they take, but they are generally slow practices. Both ethnographer and artist engage in a sustained process of working with, through and around ideas, testing out possibilities, experimenting with forms, until finally, something written that seems to make sense at the moment can be produced. This artefact, or object—a work perhaps—is open to other people's interpretations and it is only ever a partial realisation of possible meanings, a kind of temporary halt in an ongoing exploration.

This collaboration raises questions. If the research is collaborative and inter-subjective and ongoing, where does *the ethnography* begin and end? While Pat comes and goes from the Tate, as do the Schools and Teachers team albeit at different times, our conversation continues via emails, social media and exchanged documents. We wonder—if a field no longer can be seen as buildings and land—it is now also at the same time *virtual*—then what is it? If there is no recognisable site visit which is temporally boundaried, but an ongoing process of events and discussion, how are field notes to be separated from any other kind of writing that occurs?

Our view is that we write. Writing is part of how we make sense of the learning programmes on offer at the Tate. Writing began some six years ago, and goes on. This is all field. These are all perhaps then to be understood as field notes?

We have now co-written a long text, some 25000 words plus images, which we call *The Lexicon*. *The Lexicon* centres on the key words that we have found to be useful in thinking through the kind of pedagogies and learning that takes place over the immersive Summer School. Developing a shared language to talk about our understandings of gallery pedagogies has been a long project.

*The Lexicon* text takes a particular form. The writing is an attempt to be—not to 'represent'—but to *be and to do the same work* as the gallery pedagogies we describe. As such, the text is also always *a becoming*.

## 5. An extract from The Lexicon

*Learning work (a)*

> ... finding the material for learning within experience is only the first step. The next step is the progressive development of what is already experienced into a fuller and richer and also more organised form, a form that gradually approximates that in which subject- matter is presented to the skilled, mature person. (Dewey, 1938)

In gallery education, it is common for participants to have an experience—say for instance a visit to an exhibition, a lecture, a hands-on session with an artist—and then be asked to reflect on it. Materials are made available to them and these are used to reflect through making. Participants make a *work*, but the emphasis is not on the finished product. Rather, the process of making as a means of making meaning—of working through responses to and about the first learning experience—is what matters. This reflecting-making is a step towards distilling an idea, a principle, a question from the initial experience.

A question we have considered again and again is this: What is learnt when participants make a learning work? Given that we cannot peer into people's minds, we can only (1) ask them what they are thinking, (2) ask them to explain what they have made, (3) listen to their conversation, if there is any, and (4) try to *read* the object to understand what has gone on for the maker. All of these options are flawed in different ways—they are potentially intrusive and disruptive of the immediate moment or the flow of the Summer School, and they assume that making has led to a something explicit, rather than an idea/principle/question still being in formation.

We can think of the learning work as something that both produces and holds the learning. It may act as an aide-memoire for the maker or it may be discarded having done its work. It is perhaps a very mutable object (Latour, 2007), capable of performing multiple tasks for its makers and for those who look at it. We wonder how to best make sense of learning works.

We know that other people who are not part of Summer School may judge learning works harshly. They expect to see work which is polished, a finished product. A finished-with product. But the point of the learning work is that is not a finishing point. It is not a learning closure. It is some kind of disclosure—perhaps.

## Summer School 2014

The artists, Jo Addison and Natasha Kidd, asked each group to design and make a machine for noticing. This was to happen in several stages. The first stage, on Day One, was to develop a set of design principles for a noticing machine, together with some ideas about how this might look in reality. Summer School guests—architecture students—sat in with the groups and noted their discussions. Overnight they produced sketches of each group's noticing machine. These were presented to the whole group in the morning. During Day Two, each group had time to work on building a version of their *noticer*. One group finished that day. The other groups took much longer, some building more elaborate structures, one group spending all of the second day talking.

Figure 1.1: A learning work going for a walk, Turbine Hall, Tate Modern, SS 2014

On Day three, time was again made available for groups to work on their *noticer*. The group that was finished obviously had a decision to make. Would they add more to their machine? The group were unhappy with their construction. It looked, they said, amateurish, as if their primary school classes had built it, not a group of adults with some crafting skills. They decided to dismantle their construction.

Figure 1.2: Deconstructed learning work, Turbine Hall, Tate Modern

The group decision created an interesting situation/dilemma. The group had certainly exercised their agency. But on what basis was their decision made? Had they understood the *noticer-making* exercise as one primarily about making rather than the process of decision-making? In other words, did they value the product more than the process? What were the artists to do?—they could hardly make the group to more work on something they didn't see as valuable, but they also now had a group which was no longer functioning.

The artists decided to allow the group to determine its own direction; this was to proceed with individual constructions on the following days. This raised further questions about whether the problem was within the group processes, rather than the ways in which the exercise had been understood and approached.

(text written from Summer School notes, images from photographic 'daily diary')

We can perhaps think of a learning work as line of becoming, as an in between-ness happening between the materials, the space and the people concerned, and as folding the prior experience into the current. (See also *line of learning*)

Most learning works share some key features. They are:

### (1) made together

Most Summer School participants are teachers. They are used to working with students on individual projects: it is individual work that is formally assessed. They are also usually used to working by themselves, both as teachers and as artists, rather than with others. The pedagogy of collaboration in learning work encourages conversation, which helps to extend and deepen experience. But it adds another layer of experience, that of sharing a vision for making and negotiating, sparking off one another, giving up total control, enjoying *other* creativities in a non-hierarchical interaction. Some Summer School participants have found this a particularly surprising and rewarding process. Teachers and educators who participated in the 2016 Summer School were invited to return to Tate Exchange, where the school took place, to share and reflect on their learning after the event.

In the 2016 Summer School recall we were told by one participant that she had initiated and was maintaining shared video making. Another told us of a resulting partnership that worked outside school through a university-based artist-teacher programme. But more significantly, Pat's field notes each year have multiple references to participants noticing collaboration as something different, and commenting that it is something they would try in their classrooms.

### (2) made in public

For instance, in the 2015 Summer School participants worked on a joint sculpted installation in the the Tate's Duveen galleries with artist Felipe Casoblanco. Felipe had introduced the notion of *thinking backwards* from the final performance or work. A focus on the artist's intention to invite multiple dialogues and multiple perspective produced a complex structure which changed dramatically depending on the viewer's eye level and stand point.

*Figure 1.3: Group learning work with Felipe in The Duveens, Tate Britain, SS 2015*

The next day participants presented an improvised sound/image performance using materials and tools they had only encountered a couple of hours before courtesy of artist-musician Gary Stewart. The performance explored the potential for creating unexpected relationships between sound and image.

*Figure 1.4: Sound and image learning work in The Duveens, Tate Britain, SS 2015*

Both the work and the performance enacted concretely the ways in which a *direct* audience affects a work/performance regardless of whether it is static or moving.

### (3) made with scrap or cheap materials

In the 2015 Summer School participants used old magazines and photocopiers to make zines, took selfies on their phones, and used a free app on their phones to make GIFs. In 2012 Edwina Ashton gave participants loads of second hand fabrics that they used to make costumes for live performance in The Tanks at the Tate Modern.

It is possible to read the use of free, cheap and scrap materials as saying that the work that is done with them is not valuable; or that budgets are tight; or that teachers are not worth spending money on. This would be to ignore the move that contemporary artists have made against equating value of an idea/work/performance with expensive materials. It isn't *art* just because it cost a lot to make. It would be to ignore that artists often elect to use materials because they aren't considered to be 'art materials'. It would also be to ignore commitments to sustainability through minimisation of waste.

The use of simple, easy to find and purchase, largely recyclable materials in learning works is (a) to use the kinds of materials that teachers themselves are likely to be able to easily have access to; and (b) to disrupt the notion that *art materials* are limited to a given set of recognised items (paint, drawing materials, plaster, stone and similar); and (c) to focus on the thinking and talking process, not the end result. The choice of materials themselves also *teach* the benefits of thinking with and through what is readily available. It is a making and a making do.

## 6. How do we understand this kind of writing?

In thinking about *The Lexicon* as writing and as text, we have drawn on experimental ethnography, contemporary live art practice and film theory.

*From experimental ethnography we take the notion of writing as emergence.*

Experimental ethnographers such as Michael Taussig and Stephen Muecke (2014) assert that an ethnographic project should not consist of predictable stages—preliminary literature work, field work, analysis and writing a final text. This kind of work assumes distance from the world being studied. Drawing on Deleuze (2001b), Taussig and Muecke argue that ethnography is always immanent; the ethnographer is not distanced and set apart from the world, but is rather *with* the world, inseparable and always becoming with/upon/of it. The ethnographer, according to Taussig and Muecke, functions in and on the world, with it and through it, mapping their environment and thus discovering their own delimited powers and relations.

The rejection of a transcendent and unitary researcher self and the move to with/upon/of is an onto-epistemological move. This can be seen for example in Taussig's experimental magical realist work *The Magic of the State* (1997) where he is both subject and object of research, a position he holds up to ironic consideration through fiction/description.

Taussig and Muecke are not concerned with representation, as have been many anthropologists. They take writing ethnography as a texting which not only brings the ethnographer into being, but also the specific place/culture/ material world. They posit the notion of writing as emergence. Deleuze explains writing as emergence thus:

> To write is certainly not to impose a form (of expression) on the matter of lived experience ... Writing is a question of becoming, always incomplete, always in the midst of being formed, and goes beyond the matter of any livable or lived experience. ... Writing is inseparable from becoming: in writing, one becomes-woman, becomes-animal or vegetable ...
>
> (Deleuze, 1998: 1)

Taussig's understandings of emergent writing are epitomised in a *paper* about the Occupy Wall Street take-over of Zucotti Park, New York (Taussig, 2012). The *paper*, entitled *I'm so angry I made a sign*, is a mix of boxed quotations from protest signs, photographs, quotations and a past-present-tense *tour* through the park occupation over time. Taussig seamlessly combines description with reflection and analysis. He not only wanted to present and analysis of what he saw in Zucotti Park, but also are his own experiences and provoke something in the reader. At the beginning of the piece, he tells readers that he has 'inserted quotations from texts by philosophers, poets, and other people worth listening to. I don't think you will confuse them, but it's better that you do' and that 'description and analysis is a culture creating activity.' (p. 56) Together these statements clearly position the text as something intended to merge with readers. Together—writer, text and reader—will not read about culture, interrogate a representation, but actually bring culture into being.

Taussig seeks also, through/in writing, to produce and thought combined—*a spark* which can 'flash and break out of language itself, to make us see and think what was lying in the shadow around the words, things we were hardly aware existed' (Deleuze, 1995: 141). Emergent writing as espoused by Taussig seeks the surprising rather than the predictable, the disruptive rather than the affirming, anger, desire, joy and *jouissance* rather than enlightenment. It is not a representation in any stable sense of the word, as it is intended to provoke the reader into both imagining the scene at Zucotti Park while also engaging with the politics of the Occupation and Taussig's discussion of signage.

We take from this example and its wider theorisation, that our writing is inseparable from our ethnographic experiences and conversations. Together, writing contributes a cartography in which we and gallery learning (the topic with which we are concerned), the people with whom we have *participated* and *observed*, the gallery and the art works are enmeshed. Any text that we produce extends our entanglement but neither the line of thought/affect or the assemblage itself does not stop with the text. The text is perhaps a point or way stop.

*From contemporary art theory we take the notion that the meaningfulness of an art work, be it object or live, happens inbetween the viewer and work.*

To understand the role of the viewer in relation to contemporary art, it is helpful to ask, as W. J. T. Mitchell puts it, *What do pictures want?* (Mitchell, 2005). One of the common principles underpinning contemporary art is that there is no passive viewer who simply receives predetermined meanings. Rather, the viewer is a necessary participant—the art does not exist without their presence. Regardless of whether the art work is a performance or recorded event or a static object, the audience participant is always required for the work to have any meaning over and above that made by the artist (Jones, 2012). Sometimes, interaction with viewers is part of the work, sometimes, it is the emotional and physical presence of the audience that is important. At other times, it is the viewer's movement, voice that creates the *art*. At all times, a work is only sense-able as the participants engage with it (Heathfield, 2004). The experience of making meaningfulness of art happens inbetween the object or performance and the participant (Dezeuze, 2010). The art work asks a viewer to become part of it, to join with it.

Viewing an art work is to become entangled with it. As meaningingfulness, middle-grounding creates both viewer and work through their intra-action.

An archive of live art requires something particular of a viewer/participant. Live art records request re-animation. An archive of live art asks the viewer to imagine themselves participating in the actual event. The small photographic records of Christo and Jeanne-Claude's works for example ask us to re-imagine events at scale—can we *see* and perhaps wonder at the Reichstag wrapped, or *feel* what it might be to walk along the floating piers on Lake Iseo? Can we perhaps even imagine how it might be for cliffs to have their constant companions of wind and sea spray dulled by wrapping? (see christojeanneclaude.net). A viewer could of course choose to see live art photos as if they were simply postcards of someone else's experience, or they might engage with their whole bodies to inhabit their version of the events.

Animation is a kind of meeting, a halfway-ness in which the viewer blurs themselves with the archive. The archive often steers this encounter in provocative ways, leading to surprise, anger, delight, grief, joy. Viewers who cannot meet an archive in the inbetween will find it unyielding of meaningfulness and affect.

We imagine our ethnographic writing as an archive which expects something of its readers. We see this not simply as a *reader response*, a text separate from the reader—the reader response an event with a beginning and an end. Animation is a process where the reader makes affective sense with the material in front of them. And the writer's intentions and practice attempt to steer the reader in a particular direction but also blur the writer and the reader in the writing. A text can be more or less authoritarian in its intent, but the reader always interprets and produces their own embodied selves, readings, emotions and contexts with, in and through the text.

Arguably, the dominant genre of social science texts, including ethnography, steers strongly through the use of structured argument, persuasive rhetoric and meta-text (Swales, 1990; Swales and Feak, 2004). It is a directive text. To convince a reader, however, of a set of predetermined conclusions may not be what all ethnographers wish to do. Sensory and literary forms of ethnography for example (see discussion at the start of this paper), desire the reader/viewer to experience something of the same affect as the ethnographers themselves experienced. And a text that allows a reader to animate affect and senses, that seeks to become inbetween, to attain meaningfulness, may not only be written in the conventional social science genre.

*The filmic practice of montage.*

Put simply, montage is the serial presentation of images one after another (Elsaesser and Hagener, 2016). No single image is intended to stand alone. A sequence of images are a whole, a moving whole. One image follows another. Meaningfulness/affect/effect is generated by the inbetween meeting of images and the inbetween-movement-through and the viewer. The order and sequence of images offer something of the in-between-ness made by the film-maker—the viewer is invited to wrap themselves into the movement and the film-maker's experiences. Viewers make their own associations, ideas and affective responses through their engagement with the assemblage which links together past and present, now and then, here and there. Montage can have a strong realist narrative intent, or it may push for something much less explicit, something abstracted, surprising, playful or mood-creating. Our montage eschews the social realist intent of rich description, and rather seeks a more inexplicit beneath-words cumulative impression.

Montage is rather like walking through a gallery *flaneur*-like (Tester, 1994). Viewers stop at works which summon, which call for their attention (Bennett, 2010), passing by those whose desires for engagement are not of interest. And this is the way in which gallery education also occurs. Learning curators arrange a series of events, opportunities for making, opportunities to discuss, to be together, to spend time with an art work, to listen, to speak. This is not a professional development activity where a pre-existing singular narrative exists, complete with directive aims and objectives. Participants experience gallery learning as a bricolage through which they construct their own map, their own particular assemblage of engagements and inbetweens.

These homologies between cartographic writing, art and film were of interest to Deleuze (2001a). All these media involved the organisation of movements and time in an immanent ontological practice—an emergence—an emergence which does work in the world, which makes worlds, people and things. A writing practice with similar intent was developed by Benjamin (2002). We cannot compare our end work with his. But in *The Lexicon*, we share an intention.

We seek a form of writing which takes up an episodic learning practice as montage and which invites readers to connect, as they will, the material that we have 'curated', and that is important to us. We invite them to enter an ethnographic emergence ...

## 7. *The Lexicon* as failure

We *have* constructed a text that is montage. Sections of it perhaps do steer readers so that they become enmeshed with an instance, an example, an image. (How would we know this?) Yet each fragment of the text remains rather conventionally written. We have made no experiments with typeface, we have not consciously written fiction, we have not deliberately disrupted causality. In each subsection, we writers remain obdurately separate from the world that we write about, the agency we attribute to art objects does not appear to be written into *Lexicon* pages. We do not yet know how to enact a more collaborative writing between ourselves, readers and the material world.

Rather, we have produced an episodic text which hopes to invite/incite *flaneurie*—browsing, inbetween loitering (Benjamin, 2002). *The Lexicon* perhaps primarily means to and makes worlds for its writers, just as the artists' books it most resembles mean more to the artist than those who engage with them later. As we read our co-constructed text we not only remember the events we have described, but we are also propelled into continuing the conversation we broke off. The emergence that Taussig espouses, that spark that takes us elsewhere, happens *in* the writing, rewriting and rereading that the ethnographers-writers undertake.

Imagine, for example, a spirit of textual adventure that took writing as a practice immanent to the world, rather than as a detached reflection upon the world and itself. Imagine the novel possibilities for thought and action that might come with a deferral of critical distance, in pursuit of a less guarded, even reckless contamination by circumstance. Imagine ways of writing that might put ourselves more deeply at risk than what we have tried till now. What could such experiments look like, and what, if anything, might they achieve? (Pandian and McLean, 2017: 3)

We continue to experiment. *The Lexicon* is an ethnographic assemblage, an archive of a conversation. Yes. But it is not yet something which meets our ambitions. We conclude.

## References

Aarsand, P. and Forsberg, L., (2010) Producing children's corporeal privacy: Ethnographic video recording as material discursive practice, *Qualitative Research,* 10(2):249-268.

Atkinson, P. and Delamont, S., (2008) *Representing ethnography: Reading, writing and rhetoric in qualitative research*, Los Angeles: Sage.

Back, L., and Puwar, N., (2013) *Live methods*, London: John Wiley & Sons.

Bagley, C., (2009) The ethnographer as impresario-joker in the (re)presentation of educational research as performance art: Towards a performance ethic, *Ethnography and Education,* 4(3):289-300.

Behar, R., (1996) *The vulnerable observer. Anthropology that breaks your heart,* Boston: Beacon Press.

Benjamin, W., (2002) *The arcades project,* Boston, MA: Belknap/Harvard University Press.

Bennett, J., (2010) *Vibrant matter: A political ecology of things,* Princeton, NJ: Princeton University Press.

Brettell, C. B. (ed.), (1996) *When they read what we write: The politics of ethnography,* New York: Praeger.

Clifford, J. and Marcus, G., (1986) *Writing culture: The politics and poetics of ethnography,* Los Angeles: University of California Press.

Clough, P., (2009) Finding 'God' in Wellworth high school: More legitimitations of story-making as research, *Ethnography and Education,* 4(3):347-356.

Coles, R. and Thomson, P., (2016) Between records and representations: Inbetween writing in educational ethnography, *Ethnography and Education,* 11(3):253-266.

Deleuze, G., (1995) *Negotiations 1972-1990,* New York: Columbia University Press.

Deleuze, G., (1998) *Gilles Deleuze: Essays critical and clinical,* London: Verso.

Deleuze, G., (2001a) *Cinema 1: The movement image,* London: Continuum.

Deleuze, G., (2001b) *Pure immanence,* Cambridge, MA: The MIT Press.

Denzin, N. K., (1997) *Interpretive ethnography: Ethnographic practices for the 21st century,* London: Sage.

Dewey, J., (1938) *Experience and education* (1963 ed.), New York: Collier Books.

Dezeuze, A. (Ed.), (2010) *The 'do-it-yourself' artwork: Participation from Fluxus to new media,* Manchester: University of Manchester Press.

Ellis, C. and Bochner, A. P. (Eds.), (1996) *Composing ethnography: Alternative forms of qualitative writing,* London: Alta Mira Press.

Elsaesser, T. and Hagener, M., (2016) *Film theory* (second edition), London: Routledge.

Fenwick, T., Doyle, S., Michael, M., K. and Scoles, J., (2015) Matters of learning and education: Sociomaterial approaches in ethnographic research, in Bolling, S., Honing, M-S., Neumann, S. and Seele, C., (eds.) *MultiPluriTrans in educational ethnography: Approaching the multimodality, plurality and translocality of educational realities,* Bielefeld, Germany: Transcript Verlag/Columbia University Press.

Fox, N. J. and Alldred, P., (2015) New materialist social inquiry: Designs, methods and the research assemblage, *International Journal of Social Research Methodology,* 18(4):399-414.

Geertz, C., (1988) *Works and lives: The anthropologist as author,* Stanford, CA: Stanford University Press.

Heathfield, A., (2004) *Live: Art and performance,* London: Tate Publishing.

Hickey-Moody, A., (2012) *Youth, arts and education: Reassembling subjectivity through affect,* London: Routledge.

Hohti, R., (2016) Children writing ethnography: Children's perspectives and nomadic thinking in researching school classrooms, *Ethnography and Education,* 11(1):74-90.

Holland, S., Renold, E., Ross, N. J., and Hillman, A., (2010) Power, agency and participatory agendas: A critical exploration of young people's engagement in participative qualitative research, *Childhood,* 17(3):360-375.

Ingold, T., (2000) *The perception of the environment. Essays in livelihood, dwelling and skill,* London: Routledge.

Ingold, T., (2011) *Being alive. Essays on movement, knowledge and description*, London: Routledge.

Jones, A., (2012) *Perform, repeat, record: Live art in history*, Chicago: University of Chicago Press.

Lassiter, L. E., (2005) *The Chicago guide to collaborative ethnography*, Chicago: University of Chicago Press.

Latour, B., (2007) *Reassembling the social. An introduction to Actor Network Theory*, Oxford: Oxford University Press.

Maclure, M., Holmes, R., MacRae, C., and Jones, L., (2010) Animating classroom ethnography: Overcoming video fear, *International Journal of Qualitative Studies in Education,* 23(5):543-556.

Marcus, G., (2012) The legacies of Writing Culture and the near future of the ethnographic form: A sketch, *Cultural Anthropology,* 27(3):427-445.

Mills, D., and Morton, M., (2013) *Ethnography in education*, London Sage.

Mitchell, W. J. T., (2005) *What do pictures want? The lives and loves of images*, Chicago: University of Chicago Press.

Narayan, K., (2012) *Alive in the writing. Crafting ethnography in the company of Chekov*, Chicago: The University of Chicago Press.

Noblit, G., Flores, S., and Murillo, E., (2004) *Postcritical ethnography: An introduction*, Cresskill, NJ: Hampton Press.

Pandian, A., and McLean, S., (2017) Prologue, in Pandian, A. and McLean, S., (eds.) *Crumpled paper boat: Experiments in ethnographic writing,* Durham: Duke University Press.

Pink, S. (2009). *Doing sensory ethnography*. Thousand Oaks: Sage.

Rabinow, P., (2007) *Making time: On the anthropology of the contemporary*, Princeton, NJ: Princeton University Press.

Rabinow, P., Marcus, G., Faubion, J. D., and Rees, T. (2008), *Designs for an anthropology of the contemporary*, Durham: Duke University Press.

Reed-Danahay, D. (ed.), (1997) *Auto/ethnography: Rewriting the self and the social*, Oxford: Berg.

Rosaldo, R., (1989) *Culture and truth: The remaking of social analysis*, Beacon Press: Boston.

Shumar, W. and Madison, N., (2013) Ethnography in a virtual world, *Ethnography and Education,* 8(2):255-272.

Sparkes, A. C., (2009) Novel ethnographic representations and the dilemmas of judgement. *Ethnography and Education,* 4(3):301-319.

Spindler, G. D. and Hammond, L. A. (eds.), (2006) *Innovations in educational ethnography: Theory, methods, and results*, New York: Psychology Press.

Swales, J., (1990) *Genre analysis: English in academic and research settings*, Cambridge: Cambridge University Press.

Swales, J. and Feak, C., (2004) *Academic writing for graduate students: Essential tasks and skills (second edition)*, Ann Arbor, MI: University of Michigan Press.

Taussig, M., (1997) *The magic of the state*, New York: Routledge.

Taussig, M., (2012) I'm so angry I made a sign, *Critical Inquiry,* 39(1):56-88.

Taussig, M. and Stephen Muecke, S., (2014) *Sunset ethnography* https://vimeo.com/113130961

Tester, K. (ed.), (1994) *The flaneur*, New York: Routledge.

Ty, E. and Verduyn, C. (eds.), (2008) *Asian-Canadian writing beyond autoethnography*, Waterloo, Canada: Wildred Laurier University press.

VanSlyke-Briggs, K., (2009) Consider ethno-fiction, *Ethnography and Education,* 4(3):335-345.

Visweswaren, K., (1994) *Fictions of feminist ethnography*, Minneapolis: University of Minnesota Press.

White, M. L., (2009) Ethnography 2.0: Writing with digital video, *Ethnography and Education,* 4(3):398-414.

Chapter 2

# *Changing Play*—art, material play and learning

*Anton Franks*

In early childhood there is no important difference between play and work, art and science, recreation and education—the classifications normally applied by adults to a child's environment: education is recreation, and vice versa. (Nicholson, 1972: 12)

## 1. Introduction—A warm afternoon and good for playing, art and research

It's a warm afternoon in June and I am standing in an outdoor play area, a yard behind a nursery in an early childhood centre. For the moment, the yard is relatively quiet with just the background hum of the dense and diversely populated city that crowds in on the centre. The children are at lunch inside. The equipment usually laid out in the play area, has been cleared away. Instead, materials—sheets of foam, some with holes cut into them, corrugated Perspex sheets and circular mirrors, cords and clips and other assorted materials—are arranged around the yard. It doesn't look like the work of young children and I know it's not. It is instead an arrangement of *loose parts* (Nicholson, 1972), an installation of sorts, where nothing is fixed. Everything is available for the children when they venture out after their lunch. The selection of materials and their arrangement in the yard is the work of an artist, Albert Potrony. (Since Albert's project, there have been three more iterations of the project at the Portman Early Childhood Centre, each with a different artist and taking very different forms). Albert describes his approach as 'social image practice', participatory work with installation, sound and video. Important to him is the idea of 'holding a space without giving a sense of direction and allowing that direction to come from the people you're working with' (post-project telephone interview with Albert Potrony, 22 July 2017). He has been commissioned by education curators of the Serpentine Galleries, Alex Thorp and Ben Messih.

Figure 2.1: 'Loose parts' laid out ready for play in the nursery yard

The Serpentine Galleries themselves are housed in two separate buildings, situated in Kensington Gardens which adjoins Hyde Park in central London, alongside the Serpentine lake. The lake is used for swimming in summer months and the park is a place for leisurely walking, running and also for exercising horses owned by military and civilians. Both the parks and galleries are largely frequented by somewhat affluent residents and tourists. But the education programme is community-based work. The Portman Early Childhood Centre is situated north-west of the parks, in north Westminster, in which large estates of social housing predominate. The centre provides a resource for children and their families in the surrounding area. They are mostly low-income households and, although they are from a wide variety of cultural backgrounds, including East and South Asia, North-eastern and Sub-Saharan Africa, a relatively high percentage of the families (mostly mothers) are Arabic-speaking, from North Africa and the Middle East. On the ground floor of the centre, the nursery where Albert is working, is for three- and four-year-olds, with roughly equal numbers of girls and boys. Above it there are two additional floors which house a drop-in centre and crèche for parents, babies and toddlers, providing coffee mornings for families with particular interests, for example, for parents who have children with special educational needs.

Back in the nursery, Albert is assisted in the laying out of materials by the two education curators, with just a little help from me, the researcher. Albert has been commissioned to work with the nursery children by Alex and Ben. They call the project with Portman *Changing Play*, part of a larger program, *World Without Walls*, through which the education curators engage with children and young people via their schools and children's centres in this area. It is a long-term project that has involved working with a series of different artists over time. Albert has been commissioned after he and the Serpentine's education curators have spent time talking with the nursery staff and the head of the Portman.

In commissioning artists to work on the community-based projects that are part of *World Without Walls*, the education curators are careful to select artists who fit the requirements and aspirations of the nursery's children and staff. Alex is clear that projects have to be developed collaboratively and over time: "It's not for the Serpentine to develop proposals," Alex says, when meeting with her a few days earlier to talk through the project, "but to co-develop the work." She wants to avoid projects that appear to be "parachuted in" and takes time to build networks and relationships so that she might "develop familiarity with values and with the community" so that they can have "continuity and see development" through their joint projects (from initial discussion with education curators, Alex Thorp and Ben Messih, 9 June 2016).

The focus of the Serpentine's education team in promoting community based, participatory arts programs, Alex tells me, is centred on children and young people. As much as possible, they want the work to be led by them. The artist's role is to follow the children's lead, to listen and observe carefully and to provide an environment and processes to allow for development of the children in their place in the community. Four themes cut across each of the Serpentine's education projects under the banner of the *World Without Walls* program: migrations and movements; rights to the city; children's right to play; and rethinking schooling. The education curators' aspiration is to work not just with children and young people but, through them, to engage with their families and in this way to make contributions toward positive changes in the wider community. Alex is clear that her remit as an education curator is not to do *outreach* work for the gallery—it is not designed to trawl people to come to the gallery, but to firmly situate arts practice as an agent of change in the community. "The generating thing is about promoting change," Alex says, "hence the research element" (from initial discussion with education curators, Alex Thorp and Ben Messih, 9 June 2016). And that's the main reason for the research, not to take the role of the sole and detached researcher doing research *on* the people and their work (and play), but to engage in dialogue and reflection and to contribute to the research aspect that they see as integral to the *World Without Walls* program. The active, dialogic role that the education curators take in projects is a distinctive form of practice—they take a major part, participating in projects and mediating between the artists and community participants.

Working in collaboration with the staff and the artist allows them to "address issues from within a context". In an initial discussion of the research project, Alex says that it's the "ambiguity in arts practice allowing us to get in there" (from initial discussion with education curators, Alex Thorp and Ben Messih, 9 June 2016). Later, though, when this statement is reflected back to her, Alex worries about the term "ambiguity". She thinks it is too diffuse a concept and, as such, it might undermine the social activist direction of the work on the people's rights within institutions and urban settings: "The institution is not neutral … What's unusual about the [*World Without Walls*] programs is that they take a position on issues … Going into a context and listening, and then an action takes place around an issue" (discussion with Education Curator, Alex Thorp, 8 December 2017, Serpentine Gallery). If, I respond, ambiguity is more in relation to the openness in arts practices, allowing space for negotiation of meaning and dialogue through the media of arts, then it should not have to undermine the social effects and affects (Thompson, 2009) of projects. It could and should enhance the effectiveness of the arts project as an intervention.

What emerges from conversations with Alex, Ben and Albert is their sense that situated arts projects are a strongly collective enterprise, created, and developed as a changeable process through practice and dialogue, and working towards social change. A strong emancipatory ethos underlies the work, as the four strands of *World Without Walls* initiative indicate—rights to the city, migrations and movements, children's right to play and rethinking schooling. The ethos is underlined by the curators' insistence that the project should be child- and person-centred, its development guided and led by the children and their expressed interests and needs. They are idealistic but at the same time grounded in face-to-face encounters between children in their community and adults that care for them, artists and curators. One of the main aims of Albert's work is to show children, their parents and carers the potential of play by providing a variety of materials and an expansive, imaginative space for play activity. They are art projects that, in Claire Bishop's words, "tread the fine line of a dual horizon—faced towards the social field but also towards art itself" (2012: 274).

In what follows, the aspiration is to trace some of the 'fine lines' that connect participatory arts practice and play with aspirations to social change. Questions arise for me about the nature of learning and development for each of the various participants, primarily for the children, but also for others involved—the artist, the curators, the adults that work with the children and, last but not least, for the researcher. In retrospect, the roles of art-maker, player, learner and researcher appear to blur.

Typically, small children's patterns of play are multi-layered and complex—there are many interactive aspects in terms of motivation and outward activity (Sutton-Smith, 1997). Ways in which the purposes and interventions of the variously involved adults—the artist, the curators, the nursery staff, occasionally the researcher—bear on children's play activity add additional layers of complexity, complicating possible interpretations. Play activity with materials both draws from and creates a particular cultural environment for the children. Culture is a slippery concept, but in the context of this project in which the setting involves individuals and institutions, Raymond Williams has something useful to say in giving a broad and relevant definition to culture—'a *social* definition ... in which culture is a description of a particular way of life, which expresses certain meanings and values, not only in art and learning, but also in institutions and ordinary behaviour' (Williams, 1992: 41). What may be illustrated by the patterns of children's play engagement with materials provided by the artist Albert in this iteration of *Changing Play* are the ways in which thinking and feeling are intertwined in the children's play activity. They are patterns which may be referred to in Williams' evocative and somewhat elusive phrase 'structures of feeling'. These are structures that are made visible in children's play, representing 'affective elements of consciousness and relationships: not feelings against thought, but thought as felt and feelings as thought' (Williams, 1977: 132).

## 2. Methods—Ethnography, drama and narratives of *changing play* ...

How, then, to find a way into this richly complex culture of art and play situated within a nursery space? What ways are there of making sense of the processes and forms of learning that might be taking place? Clifford Geertz provided a path, as his work has done for many others, in picking up Gilbert Ryle's concept of 'thick description' (Ryle, 1968) and applying it to the interpretative description of cultures (Geertz, 1993). Following Weber in believing that humans are animals 'suspended in webs of significance', Geertz's view of culture is 'essentially a semiotic one' (Geertz, 1993: 5). So, to grasp the significance of particular cultures, one needs a thickly descriptive approach to have any chance of understanding the meanings being made in specific sites of human cultural activity. The aim of thickly descriptive ethnography is, he asserts, 'to draw large conclusions from small, but very densely facts ... to support broad assertions about the role of culture[s] in the construction of collective life by engaging them exactly with complex specifics' (Geertz, 1993: 28). Culturally orientated interpretation and explanation is not, Geertz insists, about 'discovering the Continent of Meaning and mapping out its bodiless landscape', but about 'guessing at meanings' (Geertz, 1993: 20) from looking closely at located socially organised, meaning-making activity. My approach to guessing at meaning has been through employing three main methods—participation, observation and interview.

For much of my working life, I have not been an ethnographer, however. I have been a teacher of drama and English in secondary schools and then, for more than twenty years, a teacher educator in these subjects. In common with other teachers of the subject in the UK, my concern has been to use drama as an immersive and participatory approach to teaching and learning—in other words, I am concerned to teach *through* drama as much, or if not more, than it has been to teach *about* it as an art form. In teaching drama, I have often been a participant in the drama alongside my students, attempting to understand and take my cues from them. Drama, the most explicitly social of all art forms, is a way of experiencing, encapsulating, crystallising, narrating and exploring social relations. As such, to my mind, it shares strong connections with ethnography.

Two connected implications for my account of the *Changing Play* project derive from this idea of the connections between ethnography and participatory drama. First, that it was important for me to try to be as much inside the play experience with Albert and the children as possible, to *feel* what it was like and thereby to try and understand the dynamics, intentions and desires in the process of play. As will be seen in the account that follows, working with such small children, it was in any case more or less impossible for me to remain an outside the play experience as they wanted to involve and implicate me from the outset. In the second place, play shares strong affinities with drama—it is intrinsically socially organised and physically experienced, cultural activity, drawing from many sources in the children's social and cultural environment. Participation and immersion were the primary (perhaps inescapable) methods, setting up the sessions, during the play activity and in the discussions with the centre's staff at the end of each session. From time to time, I was able to snatch up my notebook and to take notes *in situ*, but many field notes were taken just after the session and so have a reflective quality. Overall, though, the approach might properly be characterised as participant observation.

At times, however, the observational mode of being a researcher was also an important position to adopt. Important in artistic method is the activity of documentation and Albert meticulously and methodically took digital images throughout the project. In later sessions, he printed these out and showed them back to individual children and, in the last session, he invited them to come into a room, to choose images from a selection that featured them as players and he elicited narratives from them, stimulated by the images. At these moments, it was important for me just to sit back and to observe, listen and take notes.

Finally, it was important for me to try to find out about the perceptions and observations of other involved in the project. To achieve this, it is possibly more accurate to describe the process as conversation rather than formal interview, although at times this touched on attempts at semi-structured, or narrative interview. So, I talked with the curators before, after and during the project, eliciting and exploring their aims and expectations, and similarly talked with the artist, Albert, just after the project had got underway and again when his work at the centre had finished.

## 3. Every session is a mystery …

In what follows, a selection of brief illustrative vignettes is given to thicken description and to share a sense of how this *Changing Play* project with Albert developed over time. These are instances that might be viewed, not as separate events, but that are connected by threads or (again) fine lines to make a web of meaning that make up the very particular culture that Albert's work afforded. Albert's sessions were scheduled for two hours on Wednesday afternoons, after the children's lunch. Some sessions were inside the nursery room, but many were outside, weather permitting. After each session, when the children had gone home, Albert, Alex and Ben met with the team of nursery teachers and teaching assistants. Albert documented the sessions, taking still and moving digital images. Towards the end of the project, Albert shared some selected still images that showed particular children playing with the materials and talked to them about what was going on.

> Before I went to observe him working with the children, I met with Albert in a café near the nursery two days. I joined the project for the third session and asked him how it was going. "It's a mystery!" he told me. He's done participatory

work with children before, but not with children this young. He opens his laptop and speeds through images he's taken in the previous sessions, narrating with energy and enthusiasm. There are waves of activity, he tells me, ebbing and flowing, children appearing in the yard and disappearing inside. Some remaining outside for most of the session. "Every session is a mystery," he says again. The choice of materials is important to Albert—he chooses materials that are 'unknown to the children, with no narrative attached, so they wouldn't be guided into [building] particular things'

(from initial discussion with Albert Potrony, 11 May 2016, Rooftop Café, Alfie's Antique Market, London NW8).

Albert's materials laid out in the yard are now in the hands of the children. They take up the materials and engage in ever-changing patterns of play and social arrangements. From time to time, members of staff stand back on the edges and watch. From the outset, the education curators, Alex and Ben, are willingly led into play by the children. So, too, are any of the teachers and other staff who venture into the centre of action. With notebook in hand, I try at first to sit against a wall, to just be 'a researcher', to observe and not to participate. Sitting by the wall, I am at their eye-level. They are used to approaching adults, it seems. So, it takes only a few minutes for a boy to approach me. "What are you doing?," he asks. I tell him that I am enjoying watching them play. This boy, having broken the ice with this stranger, means that a cluster of children soon gathers around me. One child arrives with a clip and attaches it to my clothes. Another child licks my cheek. I stuff the notebook into my pocket and only retrieve it to scribble notes when the children shift away from me into another formation. Irresistibly, I am drawn into their play and the materials laid out by Albert feed their activity, narratives and imaginations.

*Anton:* (to child) What's all this stuff? How do you play with it? What is Albert doing?
*Child 1:* He's making it rain
*Child 2:* He's making a prison
*Albert:* Sit there (gesturing to a child)
   A child asks for something
*Albert:* What's the magic word?
*Child:* Please!

Albert, Alex and Ben continue to arrange materials around the yard.
(from field notes, 15 May 2016, Portman Early Childhood Centre)

It's not possible to be definitive in interpreting the child's reference to rain, but last week, Albert tells me, they were forced to have the session inside because it was raining. So, perhaps this is behind the reference to rain. It is speculative, but adults may have mysterious and magical powers over weather in children's minds. Albert is interested in space, thinking that it is gendered. According to him, last week indoors, the girls were more visible and assertive in their activity. Now, outside, boys' activity appears to dominate. Perhaps, one of the bigger mysteries, is how the notion of prison is prominent, particularly in boys' narrative talk accompanying their play when, for example, using cords to tie up adults or enclosing other children in cylinders made from the sheets of corrugated PVC. (It emerges again, below, in the last session, when the children are giving a narration stimulated by the images that Albert has taken of the children and their activity with the materials.) Enclosing adults, and having themselves enclosed, in cylinders made from the corrugated Perspex sheets, fastened with cord or with sticky tape is a recurring activity. The prison motif develops in the narratives that accompany the children's activity.

Figures 2.2 and 2.3: Using materials to put people 'in prison'

*Albert:* One, two, three, we can start!

He goes into a large flat cardboard box and draws out circular mirrors on Perspex and distributes them. The children pick up stuff and start to play immediately.

*Albert:* Look at that, you start already customising.

(from field notes, 15 May 2016, Portman Early Childhood Centre)

Children attach clips to their clothes and to sheets of foam, improvising costumes of various sorts. What kinds of costumes they become are partly mediated by the materials, but mostly by the children's action. As is common in small children, the desire to repeat is strong and motivates repeated and clearly visible patterns of activity (a desire still present in adults, perhaps, but more sublimated, less visible …) (Freud, 1961).

*Albert:* What are those? What are they for?

*Child:* Power Rangers!

The boy has a foam strip that he holds laterally across his chest and flaps it up and down, like wings.

*Alex (watching):* He was doing that last time

He then holds it to his nose

*Child:* It's a nose. It's a snake. It's a snail

Fifteen minutes into the session, Alex is sitting against a wall, having foam sheets arranged around her.

Figure 2.4: Alex is covered in foam sheets

*Albert:* How beautiful. What materials did you use?
> The children ignore the question.

At the same time, in the centre of the yard, a teacher is being tied up with cord by three children, with others coming and joining in from time to time. The teacher has sheets of the foam packed into her clothes and bound around her with the cord. More cord is used to capture her and, web-like, tie the materials in.

(from field notes, 15 May 2016, Portman Early Childhood Centre)

She, like Alex, has her 'natural' human shape and costume embellished by the children. The children are intently concentrated. This nursery teacher seems very relaxed and comfortable, even though she looks like an alien or an angular 'Michelin person'. The children are leading the activities and most of the adults are following, relinquishing their status as initiators of action. Roles and relationships have been shifted by the children in the pattern of activity. Regular patterns of play have been shifted too. The materials appear to have created a very particular play world, or culture of play.

A child approaches me. He has his arms through holes in foam sheets.
*Child:* I'm a zombie.
> He slowly paddles his foam 'wings'.
> Another boy sits astride a triangular shaped piece of foam, maybe four centimetres thick. There's a hole near one acute angle of the piece
> He announces that it's a Power Ranger bike.

Figure 2.5: Playing at 'Power Rangers'

A girl is bouncing a foam pipe in front of her
*Child:* Bum, bum, I'm a dinosaur ...
*Albert:* That's the moment of madness
*Anton:* (pointing) Power Ranger bike
*Albert:* That's the thing at the moment—every week there's something that
        catches on
        (from field notes, 15 May 2016, Portman Early Childhood Centre)

It is in these instances that it becomes apparent that the web of meaning that constitutes the children's particular culture of play extends beyond the boundaries of the yard in the early childhood centre. The 'ordinary behaviour' that Williams defines as a main constituent of culture is in the patterned activity and interactions of play, and the institutions include not only the immediate context of the nursery, but also the forms of media through which they are introduced to Power Rangers, zombies and dinosaurs. These characters figure prominently in the narratives the children voice as an intrinsic part of how meaning is generated for them as they play with the materials. They are, as other researchers have observed, powerful figures in the children's imaginative play (Dyson, 1997; Marsh, 2000; Burn and Richards, 2013).

Power and agency represent other aspects that emerge strongly in the instances of the children's play given above. With the stuff that Albert makes available for them—clips, cords, foam and corrugated Perspex sheets—the children are given license to exercise power over adults, tying them up, covering and attaching clips to them. They exercise and explore ideas of containment and imprisonment in solidly material form. The play is just that, play. Exploring how small children are not simply subject to adult power but are able to take power for themselves and against the adults that supervise them, Valerie Walkerdine gives an instance boys' play that might be interpreted as having some malicious intent directed at a female teacher (Walkerdine, 1993). But there appears to be nothing malicious in terms of action or intent in the ways that the children apply constraint here. It is simply what the material stuff affords them. It is done, and it passes without harm.

## 4. What grown-ups make of the art-play ...

After the session, a large circle of chairs is arranged in the nursery room. The staff are clearing away, talking to the parents and carers who come to collect the children, filling in notes for each child and, after forty minutes or so, they come to take their seats in the circle. One of the teachers is showing an image on her iPad that she's taken of two circular mirrors reflecting the sun filtering through dappled leaves. She thinks it a lovely image. The staff share observations they have made of the children's play from the periphery of the activity. Some children like licking metal. Another child likes arranging circles—he's interested in math and makes 'amazing patterns and shapes' with the materials. They observe how the children respond differently outside from when they were playing in the nursery room the previous week.

Albert agrees—he thinks the children work differently with the materials outdoors. Their action is 'very physical', he thinks, not so much 'violence' as there was last week. The head of the centre responds, telling Albert that, "Violence is quite a strong word to use about four- or five-year-olds." The conversation turns to 'play fighting' and 'rough play' and gendered differences. "Perhaps we need video ... We're missing stuff." Alex says that they have 'Go-Pro' video cameras—perhaps, they can get the children to wear them next week (from field notes, 15 May 2016, Portman Early Childhood Centre).

Reflecting on the children's patterns of play at the end of the session gives another instance of the expansive capacities of Albert's work on *Changing Play*. During the afternoon, the play was absorbing and tightly focused for me as I got drawn into the action. I scarcely noticed the staff that came, watched and departed. There were clearly aspects of the children's activity that shed new light on the children and their potentials for the staff members observing the play. Through the space afforded for observation and reflection, they were able to see the children and their creative potential in a new light, a light which would not normally be apparent to them in the normal, busy course of the working day in the nursery.

At the same time, the observations of the centre's staff were able to illuminate aspects of meaning for Albert, Alex and myself that absorption in the world of the children's play obscured for us at the time. In talking with Albert after the project, he described how the post-session reflections helped him develop the work: "Conversations with staff following sessions were very useful and led me to provide fewer materials, make holes in some [the foam], to bring in mirrors and to try taking all the materials outside." For Albert, the dialogic aspects of the project were formative:

There was dialogue between the sessions with staff, with materials, with the children via the materials. Then I could reassess. We had amasing conversations. What were things the main threads emerging from it? There was the theme of both chaos and order, expressiveness. There was also an impact on staff, the activity serving as a springboard for discussion of their own practice. Also, a dialogue between themselves and the children by changing the environment. Changing the environment led to conversations.

(Interview with Albert Potrony, 22 July 2017)

Albert's formulation of dialogue is inclusive. Again, illustrating the capacities for social interaction afforded by material stuff, he clearly suggests that the stuff itself was a powerful medium of dialogue. He suggests, perhaps, that the materials provided a means for externalised social dialogue between people, but also an internal, psychological aspect of dialogue between the materials and the thinking processes of both children and adults. Another aspect that presents itself in thinking about the relation between materials, material culture and dialogue. Material anthropologist, Daniel Miller, makes the bold claim that stuff makes the human subject as much as subjects make stuff—'objects make us, as part of the very same process by which we make them. That ultimately there is no separation of subjects and objects' (Miller, 2010: 60). It is this idea I will return to in conclusion.

## 5. Children's images and narrative ...

In the last session of Albert's project with the children, he had mounted a selection of still images that featured particular children playing with materials. Children came into a small room one at a time along with one of the nursery teachers. Albert asked the children to look at the images, to choose the ones they liked and invited them to talk about what was going on. The first child, a boy, M, gives quite a brief, formal answer when he is asked what he is doing:

M: I make 1, 2, 3 to connect to the ceiling.
*Albert:* Was it difficult?
M: I started to count it, 1, 2, 3 and connected it.
*Albert:* Why did you make it?
M: Because I wanted to.

(from field notes, 29 June 2016, Portman Early Childhood Centre)

It emerges over time that M's answer is a typical response to Albert's 'why?' questions. A little later, a girl, N, is an enthusiastic and expansive storyteller and she stays for a long time in the room telling her story. Below, she is looking at an image in which she has encased herself in a sheet of corrugated Perspex, wrapped around her in a cylinder, a circular mirror is attached to it:

*N:* I was going to space.
*Albert:* And that's the mirror. What was that for?
*N:* (more incredulity) Going to space!
*Albert:* To the moon?
*N:* And space.
*Albert:* How will you get back?
*N:* In a hot balloon … it's too little for you. When you get giant, you can see the moon. Vrooom, vroom, vroooom, going to the moon. Vrooom, vroom, vroooom, going to the moon.
*Albert:* What's it made of?
*N:* Plastic. With sprinkles on it. With a cup.
*Albert:* How do you go to space?
*N:* You make fire and go to space …
　　　　(from field notes, 29 June 2016, Portman Early Childhood Centre)

Going into space is a theme that surfaces with three of the children who take part in this part of the project. The last child to come into the room is another consummate storyteller. He is excited to see himself in the still photographs, but the stories appear only tangentially connected with the images. Towards the end of his lengthy and energetic storytelling session, H has chosen an image of himself holding one of the circular mirrors:

*Albert:* What were you doing?
*H:* I was seeing my face.
　　I was cutting my face. And broke it.
　　And then I did …
　　No, no, I went to jail.
　　I did a poo-poo on my face.
　　And let's talk about this.
　　I jumped on the face …
　　　　(from field notes, 29 June 2016, Portman Early Childhood Centre)

H was becoming more and more excited as he made his narration and was, by the end, enacting it, jumping around the room. At first glance, the images—face, cutting, jail, poo-poo—appear to be a disconnected set of icons. On reflection, however, it's clear that H is articulating a narrative that strings together images that represent the taboos of violence and scatology that he connects with his self-image. Although its psychoanalytical interpretations are tempting, I want to avoid them in this instance (how can one know about his internal worlds?) and to put an emphasis on his narrative as arising from the permissive and accepting culture of the project. He was not going to shock us, nor was he going to be admonished. Superficially, and perhaps more profoundly, he was permitted to use reflection on the materials and patterns of play as a means of (rude) expression—what those of a post-structural disposition might label as expressing a 'culture of transgression'. It is possible, though, that providing opportunity and stimulus for children to make such narratives has more positive effects in terms of children's development. Recent work in phenomenology and cognitive science has stressed the fundamental importance of narrative in 'mental time travel', that is, the ability to remember one's past and to project into the future (Hardt, 2018). It follows that the development of narrative in early childhood is key in the development of young children's emergent sense of personhood.

## 5. Conclusion: and so, to learning …

As indicated at the outset, the layered complexity of this arts project, its compressed qualities, make the task of unpacking learning a challenging one. There are many dimensions to the processes of learning involved here, so, in this concluding section, I can but point to a few indicative examples.

First, it is worth approaching what an artist such as Albert might learn from his engagement in *Changing Play*. Letting the children lead is not something that comes naturally to many adults, Alex and Ben have recognised. But they are part of the projects too, leading by example and mediating between the artist, the children and the nursery staff. In preparation for working with the children, Alex had sent Albert three published pieces—one, referred to above, architect and academic Simon Nicholson's *A Theory of Loose Parts* (1972), the other, a piece by Danish artist, Palle Nielsen (cf., Gether et al., 2015) In common between Nicholson and Nielsen are critical perspective on how adults—notably designers, architects and artists—make assumptions about children, their art and play, and impose their values when setting up play spaces rather than being led by the children and young people. Later, Alex passes on a chapter, 'Towards a pedagogy of listening', from Gunilla Dahlberg and Peter Moss' book, *Ethics and Politics of Early Childhood Education* (2004) to support Albert in understanding the importance of listening. Before this project, Albert had worked with children, but not such young ones, and that had been in drop-in sessions in a gallery.

Later, when I speak to him after the first phase of *Changing Play*, Albert reflects on the journey he had taken so far on the project. First, I ask him how he felt about Alex and Ben's involvement:

> Basically, this constellation of constant checking up what's going on, trying collectively trying to make sense, feeding each with other things. I would try things and Alex sort of would come across. I thought that was really rich in this project. I had very good working relationships with other curators, and really fashioning things together. But in this case, it was not just the curator but also the staff, almost even the children in a non-verbal way. Just being aware of what was happening and changing things because of that.
>
> (Interview with Albert Potrony, 22 July 2017)

For Albert, the project was a kind of journey of discovery, informed by the children's play itself, discussions with nursery staff and education curators that went on through the project and, in the background, his repeated reading of the work Alex had sent him:

> To think back and looking and following, quite a discovery in a way. Yes, I was there and, somehow, I was meant to be leading it, but also, I was being led. I was mainly being led by what was happening. Yes, at the beginning, it was slightly vertiginous, but it was also very exciting. It helped me look more instead of assuming …
>
> (Interview with Albert Potrony, 22 July 2017)

Here, Albert returns to the theme of dialogue, albeit somewhat obliquely. What he describes in terms of leading or being led is not necessarily a smooth and easy process of agreement. Tensions and dissonances may appear. Yet, as Richard Sennett observes, dialogue involves 'discussion which does not resolve itself by finding common ground … The players do not sound exactly on the same page, the performance has more texture, more complexity, but still the players are sparking off each other' (Sennett, 2012: 19-20). Eventually, Sennett claims, dialogue eventually can result in mutual understanding. There is a sense here of understanding, and more than that, that the project has been a process of learning for Albert.

There are implications here, too, for the work of the Serpentine's education curators, Alex and Ben. In their insistence that the work is not outreach but is community-based, taking artists and art-making into the community, they open a dialogue between artists, the gallery and groups in the community. Their work is concerned with the rights of immigrant communities, such as the Arabic-speaking members of the community who comprise a significant segment of the local population and whose children attend the early childhood centre, the right to participate fully in the life of the city having access to its resources, to have a rich and developmental play environment for their children and to have fullest possible access to education. In the area of education, for example, they promote creative child-centred, approaches, and especially for the inclusion of children with different and particular needs. The early childhood centre is not a simple location, it is a hub around which children, parents, staff and other members of the community revolve. In so doing, they extend the boundaries and therefore the civic responsibilities of the gallery. Whether or not the gallery is able to learn and develop from this point is a moot point, but the capacity for extending the work of the gallery beyond its walls is there.

The work of the Serpentine's education team extends further beyond the locality, however. Later, Alex writes to me about how she would want to talk about the potential impact of their work with children and families beyond the specific community. She writes to me:

I think it's important to acknowledge that a toolkit was produced in cooperation with the Portman, designed to generate critical conversations about early years practice with practitioners and parents beyond the immediate community. We've handed out close to 200 toolkits so far. We have also consciously situated the debate within the current context of school readiness: As Ofsted introduces the controversial *Bold Beginnings* (2017) report, which places emphasis on formal education over play, we invite early years practitioners to question the schoolification discourse and re-imagine what it means to be ready for school. The toolkit is designed to support teachers in forming solidarities with the children they work. How can we prepare schools for children? How can we support play in early years education?

(Email from Alex Thorp, 27 September 2018)

At the centre of the frame, however, there must also be a way of approaching and interpreting children's learning. A culturally situated and culturally mediated perspective on play, learning and development as being can be found in the work of Lev Vygotsky and subsequent elaborators of his work. Vygotsky regarded the imaginative play of pre-school children as providing a cultural environment that leads development.'As in the focus of the magnifying glass, play contains all the developmental tendencies in a condensed form and is itself is a major source of development' (Vygotsky, 1978: 102). Thus, play creates what Vygotsky refers to as a 'zone of proximal [or next] development' through its facility for creating and enhancing imaginative, meaning-making activity. In thinking about the development of the capacity for imagination, Vygotsky suggests that the old adage that play in children is imagination in action needs to be thought of in reverse—namely, that imagination in adults is play without action (Vygotsky, 1978: 93).

Imagination is just one aspect of development that emerges through children's play, however—another key aspect is how Vygotsky explains that the meaning-making, symbolic aspects of play are a precursor to literacy. This is evident in the vignettes given above both in the narratives that children make that accompany play, and in the narratives that are stimulated when Albert invites them to talk about the images. Initially, nursery staff were sceptical of the children's capacity to remember events and of their ability to sustain narratives. The different stages of *Changing Play* with Albert allowed them a deeper understanding and appreciation of children's capacities for making narratives and in approaching literacy.

Finally, another key aspect of learning and development that deserves more consideration (than available space here allows) is how such community-based arts work feeds into the of children's developing sense of personhood. Another key concern related to the development of agency and personhood in young children, is the role that playing and making art with stuff may have in preparing them to take an active place within wider social institutions beyond the nursery environment. A topic important to the staff that arose in post-session discussions revolved around the role and responsibilities of the nursery in helping the young children prepare for entry into formal schooling, the issue framed in terms of 'school readiness'. One aspect of helping children get ready for school is providing preparation for the demands of the curriculum, such as literacy and numeracy. Another major aspect of this discussion, however, is a concern with preparing the children to become school students, subject to the institutional demands and rigours of schooling. Locked into these concerns is a sense of responsibility that the staff have for bolstering children's *resilience* so that they might be able to navigate and survive such rigours. One way of understanding the concept of resilience in this context is as a somewhat negative capacity—resilience as an adaptation of compliance, an adaptation that allows survival of the person and their personhood in the face of societal and institutional pressures of oppression and injustice (Rogers Hall and Salamanca, 2017). Rogers Hall and Salamanca suggest that, instead, resilience should be understood 'as something that arises from resisting with dignified anger' (Rogers Hall and Salamanca, 2017, 124). Another possible way to think of resilience, however, is as a capacity may be fostered through the joy of creative activity. Seen in this light, the involvement of the young children in the work of *Changing Play* with Albert, Alex and Ben may do much to assist the development children's creative capacities, which in turn may contribute to developing their sense of agency and personhood.

For Alex, listening and observing children and those that surround and care for them, are radical acts. It is evident in their insistence that the children should be allowed to take the lead. The ways in which such a community-based arts project with young children acknowledges and facilitates their sense of agency and offers resources is evident in the free-wheeling creativity of their play with materials and the narratives that they construct. Miller's suggestion that stuff makes people as much as people make stuff is perhaps only part of the story. It is the patterns of activity, what they do with the stuff they play with, and how adults can assist and feed their play that is key in assisting development of these young children through art and play.

## Acknowledgements

The research that serves as a source for this chapter is funded by the Sackler Family Trust. Permissions have been sought and granted to name the site of research, the Portman Early Childhood Centre, as well as the Serpentine Galleries and its Education Curators, Alex Thorp and Ben Messih, and the artist, Albert Potrony. The writing of this chapter has been substantially informed by discussion with Professor Pat Thomson, School of Education, University of Nottingham, UK, the Principal Investigator of this evaluation research project with Serpentine Galleries Education.

# References

Bishop, C., (2012) *Artificial hells: Participatory art and the politics of spectatorship*, London: Verso.

Burn, A. and Richards, C., (2013) *Children's games in the new media age: Childlore, media and the playground*, Burlington: Ashgate.

Dahlberg, G. and Moss, P., (2004). *Ethics and politics in early childhood education*, London: Routledge

Dyson, A. H., (1997) *Writing superheroes: Contemporary childhood, popular culture, and classroom literacy*, New York: Teachers College Press.

Freud, S., (1961) *Beyond the pleasure principle*, London: Hogarth.

Geertz, C., (1993) *The interpretation of cultures: selected essays*, London: Fontana.

Gether, C., Høholt, S., Juul Rugaard, D. and Jalving, C. (eds.), (2015) *Palle Nielsen: The model*, Ishøj, Denmark: ARKEN Museum of Modern Art.

Hardt, R., (2018) Storytelling agents: why narrative rather than mental time travel is fundamental, *Phenomenology and the Cognitive Sciences*, 17(3):535-554.

Marsh, J., (2000) 'But I want to fly too!': Girls and superhero play in the infant classroom, *Gender and Education*, 12:209-220.

Miller, D., (2010) *Stuff*, Cambridge: Polity.

Nicholson, S., (1972) The theory of loose parts, *Studies in Design Education Craft & Technology*, 4:5-14.

Ofsted, (2017) *Bold Beginnings*, London: HMSO. Accessed: https://schoolsweek.co.uk/wp-content/uploads/2017/11/28933-Ofsted-Early-Years-Curriculum-Report.pdf

Rogers Hall, K. and Salamanca, M., (2017) Relocating precarity and resiliency within Montreal: the Artists' Bloc of the Immigrant Workers' Centre, *Research in Drama Education: The Journal of Applied Theatre and Performance*, 22:116-125.

Ryle, G., (1968) *The thinking of thoughts (University of Saskatchewan Lectures, n° 18)*, Saskatoon, SK: University of Saskatchewan.

Sennett, R., (2012) *Together: the rituals, pleasures & politics of cooperation*, London: Penguin.

Sutton-Smith, B., (1997) *The ambiguity of play*, Cambridge: Harvard University Press.

Thompson, J., (2009) *Performance affects: Applied theatre and the end of effect*, Basingstoke: Palgrave Macmillan.

Vygotsky, L. S., (1978) *Mind in society: The development of higher psychological processes*, Cambridge: Harvard University Press.

Walkerdine, V., (1993) Sex, power and pedagogy, in Alvarado, M., Buscombe, E. and Collins, R. (eds.), *The screen education reader: Cinema, television, culture*, London: Macmillan Education.

Williams, R., (1977) *Marxism and literature*, Oxford: Oxford University Press.

Williams, R., (1992) *The long revolution*, London: The Hogarth Press.

# Chapter 3

## Creative teaching practices of art in education in rural schools

*Maria Begoña Vigo Arrazola and Dennis Beach*

### 1. Introduction

In Spain art has been a common way for schools to individualise the curriculum to the needs of their pupils. In this chapter, based on an analysis of an ethnographic research in a small rural school in Spain, we will try to begin to develop and deepen understandings of how the arts can be put to work in order to facilitate the participation and learning of pupils in contexts where classroom heterogeneity predominates. In rural schools in each classroom there will most likely always be a mix of ages, abilities and disabilities, cultural backgrounds and also often these days parent nationalities and languages. Although not unique, as this happens elsewhere too, rural schools are usually very special in these respects. They are *incomplete*, *mixed-aged* and *mixed-grade* schools where there is no possibility for composing special classrooms for children with special intellectual challenges or from different linguistic backgrounds.

The predominance rather than merely the presence of different cultures is usually the rule rather than the exception in many of these schools at the present time. This was certainly the case in the school we have been involved with. Using other forms of expression than the standard written and national formal/official language was therefore common and several different studies have shown the relevance of media such as animation and the arts in order to create positive experiences that can contribute to building relationships between children from different language backgrounds and cultures, to increase their understandings of content and of others (Hickey-Moody, 2017). These studies highlight the benefits of art integrated with curriculum concepts to contribute to promote cognitive skills and the development of vocabulary, reasoning, and abstraction (Baker, 2013) as well as literacy and math whilst also nurturing art making skills, creativity, and the ability to meaningfully reflect on one's own work and that of peers. These practices have been highlighted as particularly useful in schools for children from poor communities (Cunnington, Kantrowitz, Harnett, and Hill-Ries, 2014).

Thus, we are far from alone in relation to our interests in the value and potential of art across the curriculum in educationally challenging circumstances. In our examples, art is used to stimulate free thoughts and associations as a foundation for free production and open discussions and attempts were made by educators to consciously grasp the heart, memories, experiences and emotions of their pupils and to channel their developing reflections toward intellectual labour that crossed cultural borders and allowed learning experience to connect with everyday life.

## 2. Theory and method

In this chapter, in terms of theory, we are looking at material and cultural-historical definitions of art, where art is associated with being creative to the solution of particularly experienced problems, or as put by Paulo Freire, we are exploring the use of art and creativity as a means to encourage reflection and action upon the world in order to transform possibilities within it (1972/2000). What we mean here is that we are aiming to analyse art in the curriculum as a form of creativity that develops dialectically and where what is accepted as creativity is broadened and contextualised as an attribute of the particular social and material conditions.

Everyone has the capacity to be creative from this perspective, at the same time as contexts and situations have the capacity to dull, silence or alienate that creative potential (Hay and Kapitzke, 2009; Lundberg, 2015). In a place such as the currently often negatively represented small urban peripheral or poor rural school it means that creativity will be present and can be identified in different ways.

We are then operating from a departure in relation to a dialectical and materialist concept of creativity as an ability to engage in real processes of production. As expressed by Marx in the German Ideology such a dialectical and materialist conception of creativity starts out from considering the material production of life itself and comprehending the form of intercourse connected with this and created by this mode of production (i.e. civil society in its various stages). It then describes this history in terms of its actions and sets out to explain and understand all the different theoretical products and forms of consciousness that derive from it, such as religion, philosophy, ethics, and similar displines, tracing at the same time their origins and growth from their basis in the conditions of production in terms of a totality. Thus there is also a focus on the reciprocal action of these various aspects of culture on one another. The terms cultural-historical and historical-materialist analysis are often used to describe this perspective.

In addition to adopting a dialectical cultural historical perspective, our chapter fits into an ethnographic research tradition and applies it to research on creative practices in Education. Work by Woods (1993), Woods and Jeffrey (1996), Craft (2002) and Jeffrey and Troman (2009) use ethnography in a similar way but from a symbolic interactionist perspective. Our work likens thus more that of Beach and Dovemark (2007). It considers creative teaching practices as a part of material reality and sets out to contribute to understanding the sense of art connected with an education for all and the complexity of lived educational situations in difficult circumstances. Relevance, ownership of knowledge, control of learning processes, innovation and social transformation are itemised aspects (Woods and Jeffrey, 1996; Jeffrey, 2006; Troman and Jeffrey, 2007).

*Relevance*: Learning that is meaningful to the immediate needs and interests of pupils and to the group as a whole.

*Ownership of knowledge*: The pupil learns for himself / herself—not the teacher's, examiner or society's knowledge. Creative learning is internalised and makes a difference to the pupil's self (Vigo and Soriano, 2014).

*Control of learning processes*: The pupil is self-motivated, not governed by extrinsic factors, or purely task-oriented exercises.

*Innovation*: Something new is created, a new skill mastered, new insight gained, new understanding realised, new, meaningful knowledge acquired.

*Transformation*: A major change has taken place where a radical shift is indicated, as opposed to more gradual, cumulative learning.

Considering these definitions of creativity, art can be used as a form of expression through drawing, writing, music and other similar media, and as a way to enable children who often have marginal command of the formal language codes (in this case school, Spanish) and little previous formal schooling as a way to communicate interests, perceptions of the world, knowledge and understanding and learning needs. It allows pupils and teachers to connect their experiences, environment and life within the curriculum through processes of expression, exchange and cooperation that might not otherwise take place so easily in relation to school knowledge, if at all. In this chapter we explore what characterises the repertoire of action in teaching and learning situations using art to such ends. We will also consider the potential shown (or blocked) for curriculum engagement with the possibly contradictory, deviant, and generative forms of knowledge that are embedded within social reality.

## 3. Research context

Lythe School (a pseudonym) is a small rural school in Aragon, Spain, located in a peri-urban space on the rural outskirts of a small town in an agricultural municipality. It has two classrooms only and its pupils come from families that mainly work as unskilled labourers in the agricultural sector: in some cases on the land and in others in canning and food and wine processing industries. Each classroom has one full-time teacher and shares specialist teachers in subjects like Physical Education with other schools. There were fifteen pupils on role when the investigations started but the number fluctuated in relation to seasonal in and out labour migration across the first two years of the main study and this fluctuation persisted in the subsequent two years. At our most recent visit, in May 2017, there were twelve pupils on role in the two classrooms.

The two class teachers at the school are permanent teachers. They have been employed at the school for fifteen (primary class) and four (infant class) years respectively. The infant classroom has children from three until seven year- old and the primary has children from eight to twelve years-old. Classes are from nine o'clock to two o'clock. Every Friday, througout the day, both classrooms work together in the Library on creative projects linking the Arts and Natural Sciences on some days and Arts and Spanish on others and we have concentrated our present analysis on data we collected in this context. We have focused on creative teaching practices in these special circumstances (but also at other occasions as well) on how art was used as a way to facilitate participation and learning and to attend to individual learners and their education needs and interests.

The investigation is a regional one, and forms part of a national research and development project exploring the construction of children's involvement in rural schools. These projects were initially carried out between 2008 and 2011 in the *Evaluation and methodology: Basis to improve teaching in an inclusive rural school* project [grant number 262-101] project and the *Improvement of teaching and learning in a rural school from a creative perspective* project [grant number 262-103]. Some extension projects have been added to the research since then with the aim being to (a) further our knowledge of children's participation in school using Art practices and (b) understand the practices and experiences that teachers promoted.

The fieldwork has been carried out using participant observation, interviews, informal conversations, photography and document analysis. The interviews and conversations took place at the school and also in non-institutional environments, such as restaurants and cafés, outside school time. Following Woods and Jeffrey (1996) our intention was to examine the relevance, ownership of knowledge, control of learning processes and innovation within these processes in the classroom. This included a review of how teachers and children experienced this participation. The teachers expressed that they wanted to involve the heart and the intellect of the children in their classrooms. They said also that they felt that art was able to overcome social distance caused by linguistic difficulties and other complications when it came to trying to create educational meaning and learning.

## 4. Results

The results suggest that art was used by teachers as a space where children's participation and learning could be developed and investigated. This suggests that in terms of classroom production, teachers tried to promote free expression and interpretation as vehicles for inclusive learning through writing, art or drawing activities that were related to the life experiences of their students. They did this by involving parents and other pupils to provide support for the pupils' learning. They also tried to engage families and the community. Art was a strategy and a space of participation, expression and acknowledgement that was felt able to (and did) give voice to a sense of meaning, identity, knowledge and respect for the pupils, the families of the pupils, and the places they came from. Acceptance, participation and giving voice were very important aspects according to the teachers.

### 4.1. Voices through the arts: Relevance and acceptance

The teachers regarded art as able to extend participation and give voice as introduced in the section above to be important. It was meant to overcome possible senses, forces and effects of alienation, and to enhance possibility thinking and facilitate the participation of children from different educational levels. It was a way to try to 'incorporate everyone into the dynamics of classroom interaction' (Teacher). As expressed in fieldnotes:

Free expression and free interpretation were present and the everyday life of students was able to enter into and be registered as a contribution to knowledge in the school. Positive emotions were shown by the children when they were involved in activities such as the 'art in my country' and they say 'I like this because I am thinking of my mum'. 	(Fieldnotes, May 2017).

Emotions like the one expressed here were seen to develop from interactions in the creative activities of the collective arts lessons and to be an important aspect for teaching and learning. However, at the same time, through the engagement with their emotions the children felt able to take charge of their own learning within the formal context of the school. Again, this seems to challenge the forces that pull learning toward deeper alienation and external determination and is in line with Woods and associates reflections on creative schools and creative teaching and learning practices. As Woods and O' Shannessy (2002) put this, the more passionate children feel about learning, the more the receptive they are and the more heightened is their level of awareness.

Free expression was a common strategy in the two classrooms and we could regularly see how children combined writing and drawing showing their life in a classroom with children from Preschool and Primary Education, from three to seven years old, while the teacher facilitates and reinforces situations of free expression and free interpretation, without pre-established criteria for expression provided by the teachers (see Figure 3.1).

One girl with significant difficulties in Spanish and one boy, each from second year of primary education, started to write a story from a picture. Each one draws a scene. While one is painting, the other one begins to write the story. The girl starts and the boy supports her with comments and questions. The dialogue, the exchange of proposals and the adaptation between them are a fact. Subsequently, the written story is read and improved with the teacher. At recess, the authors decide to read it to all the children and school teachers. They listen intently first to the girl and then to the boy, looking also at the pictures they have drawn. Their classmates are the protagonists of an invented story. After reading, the questions of teachers and children, as well as responses from authors and other children, are used to improve the final story. Aspects such as reading, literature, writing or numbers are included in the intended curriculum.

(Fieldnotes, 17 May 2011. Space of infant classroom/within the schoolyard)

Figure 3.1: Collaborative free expression

What is suggested here is that students with different levels of ability and school experience and different needs and interests were able to interact freely and express what they think. However, children were also seen and treated as a person and as an active subject in these interactions and this freedom for involvement, input and interpretation seemed to be also strengthened in some situations. Free interpretation was facilitated in the classroom through drawing sometimes, or through language in others. In one case, the two classrooms were working together and teachers invited children to tell the group about their feelings about pictures that had been painted by Zurbarán (a Spanish painter) (see Figure 3.2). In terms of production and experiences, relevance through drawing can be seen in the extract below and Figure 3.2 following the extract. These examples suggest something of how art facilitates participation and the learning possibilities of the students at their own level.

> Taking as a reference the *still life (el bodegón)*, a picture from Zurbarán, each child produces another picture from his or her free interpretation. They have to draw the things each one saw. We can see how there are none exactly the same. All of them are different. Each one has a style and each emphasises a different aspect. We can see how each child perceives the picture / ... / The teacher said: "Each person has different perceptions of the real world and each picture is different because there are not two people who are in exactly the same. Each person has different perceptions of the real world" (Informal conversation with one teacher). / ... / In a spontaneous way one boy says: "I like the poster of fruits to know what day we have to eat fruit. So we always remember. On Friday we have fruit" (Pedro José). (Field notes 19 December 2008. Library, infant and primary classroom together)

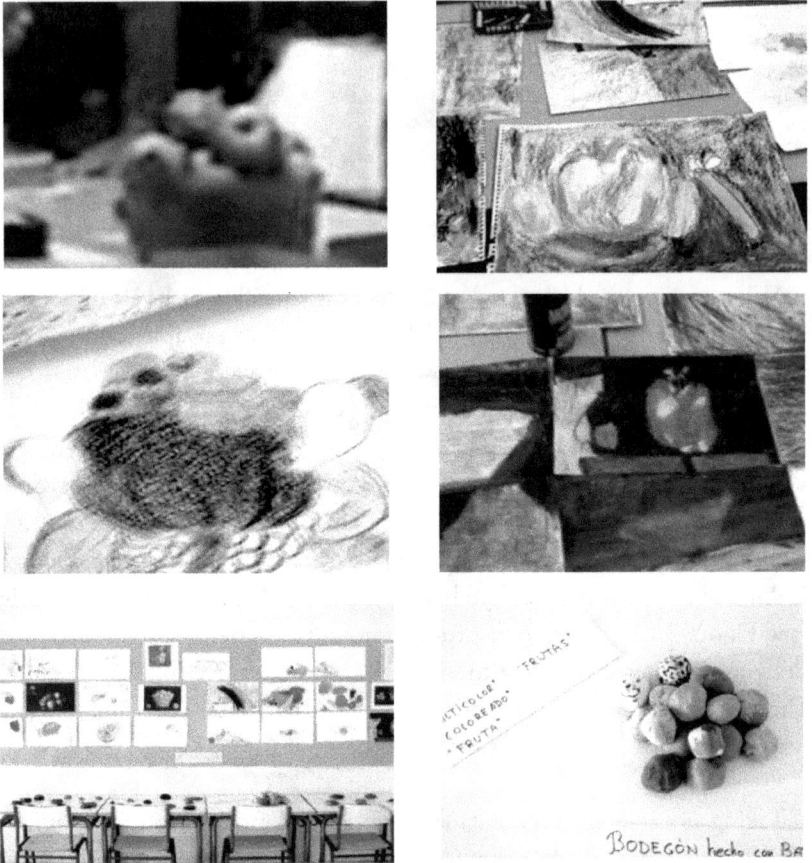

Figure 3.2: Individual interpretation and representation

The experiences of the pupils outside the school added reinforcement to the relevance and helped render meaningful connections to learning at a realistic level connected to the immediate needs, interests and life of pupils and to the group as a whole. Pupils learned for themselves through Art and creative learning was internalised and able to make a difference to the pupils' self-concepts.

### 4.2. Relevance and ownership

The fieldnotes and other documents (our photographs, our sketches and other recordings) showed how with regularity both teachers tried to promote the ownership of the knowledge through art by firstly acknowledging that each learner would quite likely learn differently and then secondly by trying to ensure that their approach was flexible enough to be relevant to all learners and their differences. Teachers tried to be flexible about the attention to the possibilities of the art they chose to use and they invited the pupils to be innovative through the art they chose in their productions. The pupils then showed how the materials and pictures can be used and interpreted. The primary teacher explained to us how much the children had learned.

> This boy (referring to a boy that did a drawing), when he arrived and I asked him to draw his dad and his mum, he told me "I don´t know, I don´t know," I just achieved that he drew a little drawing on the corner of the paper. Now, he is interacting in another way. / ... / The interaction between teachers and children and between children is continuous in the classrooms. Teachers reinforce the initiatives of the children extending and developing their proposal (21 December 2008, Informal conversation in the Library) ... While the Primary teacher is speaking with me looking at the boy she says: "You should think about the shades". After that she continues telling us "these pictures are related to Zurbarán but they are painting as they want, with light."
>
> (19 December 2008. In the Library)

What is suggested here shows empathy and subjectivity, which were expressed as fundamental to learning by the teachers. They told us time and again, how they wanted to put the children' emotions and subjectivity at the centre of the learning activities. The value of emotion and feeling are positively recognised and given space in the curriculum and this is also done often in connection with real life issues.

> To me what I like in this activity of the alphabet and numbers is to help Juliana and Ciprian, two children from Romania, to learn Castilian. We obtained a diploma and really enjoyed ourselves. "The little ones really liked the drawings we did".
>
> (Luis, 21 May 2009, in the Infant classroom)

Tasks like writing a text, the selection of a picture, or the composition of a model promoted creative energy in children according to our fieldnotes. Teachers tried to reinforce language learning through art as they felt that 'the children can express what they think from their own level, with the vocabulary they know'. (Infant Teacher).

## 4.3. Relevance and learning control through the language

Art has often been associated with the enhancement of learning possibilities and experiences for pupils with special educational needs. Indeed pupils with specific educational needs or new children from other countries who have recently moved to the school and the county. The idea is that these pupils can participate in the dynamic of the classroom through arts and the teachers in the present investigation certainly seem to be committed to this idea. But this is not intended as involvement for its own sake. As one teacher put it, by becoming involved the children also became more confident and aware of learning. We identified this in different situations in the classroom that allowed the children to express their thoughts and teachers to help them recognise that several answers to the same task could be correct.

> Today is Friday and all the children are together in the library for assembly. One teacher asks the children to remember the rules to participate in a communication process. The projector is showing the picture *La bañista* by Miró and teachers ask children what they are watching … Children exchange sentences and vocabulary according to their levels and their interests. The two teachers encourage them to participate through reinforcement. Teachers note their explanations and assess their various answers.
>
> (Field notes, 21 November 2008. In the Library infant and primary classroom together)

What is expressed here is a sense here of how teachers created climates of anticipation and expectation (Woods and Jeffrey, 1996) where children were able to freely reflect, analyse, hypothesise, identify and search for solutions to problems according to their own interests and capabilities. Teachers encouraged free expression by offering each child the opportunity to engage more actively with others, and by giving each child more space to ask their own questions and make their own discoveries (see Figure 3.3). Listening to each other became very important. Each answer was tested and repeated by the teachers, recognising each child's contribution and giving the word to them all in turn. One example occurred when teachers used paintings to stimulate reflection and conversation (as in Fig 3.3 below).

Figure 3.3: Questioning and discovering around a painting

*Edgar (11):* I see the moon reflected on the water.

*Infant teacher:* in the water?

*Edgar:* yes

*Infant teacher:* do you see the reflection?

*Edgar:* No, it is the water with the reflection.

*Infant teacher:* but ... we are going to see ... the reflection. Do you see it?...
You say "I see the moon reflected on the water"

*Edgar:* No, I see that it is the reflection.

*Infant teacher:* you see that it is the reflection. You do not see the moon. So, we have to know what we want to say.

...

*David:* I see several people and the sky yay! How do you say it?, it seems a picture ...

*Infant teacher:* a picture, several people ... So, in plural.. how do you see?

*David:* Two. I see the head and another reflected.

*Abril:* It is possible to see white things.

...

*Infant teacher:* They are stars. Why do you think that they are stars?

*Edgar:* Because the stars are white.

*Infant teacher*: Are they white, the stars?
*Edgar*: Well, they are yellowish.
*Infant teacher*: ... María what do you see sweetie?
*María (3)*: the moon
*Infant teacher*: the moon!!! Do you see anything else María?
(Field notes, 21 November 2008. In the Library infant and primary classroom together)

We can see and sense the presence here of an inclusive learning environment that is being used as a means to nurture children's creativity through the use of possibility thinking and co-participation (Craft and Jeffrey, 2004). The children are encouraged to pose questions, identify problems and discuss ideas together. There is an opportunity an opportunity to debate and discuss their thinking. These are all ways to bring the learner into the process of possibility thinking as co-participants (Craft and Jeffrey, 2004) and through them the classroom is transformed as a space for exchanging ideas and proposals that contribute to the actual design and development of learning content. In the sense of Bernstein (1990), we could perhaps speak of an open classification and framing. The pupils engage with enthusiasm and enjoyment in the activity. They describe many enjoyable experiences.

*Abril*: I have been many times on the beach playing.
*Juanjo (8)*: One day I went with my father on the beach; then we went to the lighthouse ...
*Infant teacher*: ohhh ... ¡the beach has a lighthouse!... very good ... .Pedro José ... what picture do you choose?
...
*Primary teacher*: I like it, and because it is very nice. I have the sensation that it never ends and there is always something to see ... It is the water. It is the line of the horizon on the picture, the clouds with the little things that there were, and the waves ... There is ...
*Nico*: I have been on the sea but my parents do not want me to swim there
(Field notes, 21 November 2008. Infant and primary class in the Library)

Co-participation is constructed here as a way in which the learner can be included in the sharing and creation of knowledge. This kind of inclusive learning environment might be considered to exemplify a good teaching tool because it reflects and acknowledges the contribution of all. The experience and backgrounds of the pupils and their lives and origins are considered to be important foundations for and potential drivers of classroom learning as a way of reinforcing personal history in school activities in the sense of Woods and O' Shannessy (2002). The interactions that took place helped the pupils to advance from one level of learning to the next and to become aware of their learning.

The role of the teacher in the form of learning that characterised the use of art was the role of a facilitator combined with that of a mediator in an environment that valued the child as a person (see Figure 3.4). The exchange of ideas between children of different ages, cultures and educational levels and between teacher and children enabled individual and social enrichment and there was a clear personal (learner/individual) centred orientation of pedagogy as expressed in for instance the pedagogical philosophy of Carl Rogers from the 1970s. Free writing and painting and free interpretation were used as creative teaching and learning strategies that contributed to inclusive practices. Children could express an individual interpretation of the world in which they live, by considering their needs, interests, experiences of home, family, movies or the products of their imagination. Their voices were present and there were affective aspects in these voices. Children could give voice to and find a place to develop their interests. Experiences of home, family, movies or the products of their imagination were all given a place in the curriculum.

Figure 3.4: Material representation: Environment, Art and life

## 4.4. Heart and intellect: Acceptance and exchange

The previous sections illustrate in several ways how Art was used in one rural school to foster individual expression and promote creative learning by enabling children to bring their experiences from outside the school into the school context (Vigo and Soriano, 2014). Art was a way to create a special communication interface in the classroom. It helped the teachers to get to know the pupils and to help them to express and use their knowledge as the basis of learning in subjects like the Spanish language, mathematics and science. The realities and interests of the pupils thus actually led curriculum development and reflected the teachers' beliefs that every child arrives at school with a set of valuable experiences that can become a connecting point or an axis for articulating individual action. However, the selection of an image, drawing or the interpretation of a picture by a child also promoted creative energy for the pupils for further sharing reflections, analyses, hypotheses and searches for solutions to the problems they identify and experience. Far from being static and alien to their experiences, art reinforced a curriculum tailored to the heterogeneous experiences of the population in the contents of Language, Mathematics, Science or Geography. Moreover, communication between the teacher and the children, and between the children themselves, also allowed the children to become more self-motivated.

A starting point in all of this was the acceptance of pupil value. It involved a direct negation of the standard classically bourgeois curriculum inherited by the formal school and enabled individual and social enrichment of a kind that was able to overcome the kinds of objectification, deindividuation, and routinisation of emergent educational realities in conventional schooling. There was cooperation based on familiarity and a sense of a joint purpose that marked out an articulation of personal learning in the classroom and the school. Respect for the original thinking of the child promoted mutual interchanges where pupils were also given free space to learn to think and make intellectual judgements on their own comments, questions or issues. In this sense, the interactions that are promoted in the school through art integrated learning also facilitated the diagnosis, evaluation, transformation and evolution of the pupils in different situations and contexts.

This broadening of the basis of familiarisation and assessment provides significant information about the functioning of the institution in relation to social reality and child identities and creative teaching, which also becomes a means of addressing the needs of a school characterised by heterogeneity, considering ethnic, religious, linguistic, gender and to some degree even class differences, which were though much smaller except between teachers and pupils' parents, as the children came in class terms from a common background of a trans-local and mobile agricultural physical labour force. Broadening familiarisation was a way of taking creative teaching to work with pupils whose learning is at different levels of development that takes both individual needs and the demands of administration into account (Jeffrey, Troman and Philipps, 2008). The teachers connected the work in the classroom with the reality outside school, they made less use of the textbook and they carried out different activities of expression and communication, connecting the objectives of these activities with the curriculum requirements proposed by the school administration. Creativity was not limited to the Arts only. It was also connected with language, natural sciences or mathematics.

*Sara (5):* I see another line but one with colour
*Infant teacher:* So, what is this line Sara?
*Sara:* A curve.
*Infant teacher:* A curve! ahhh ... so, the other black line? What was it?
*Raúl:* A curve.
*Infant teacher:* Was it a curve also Raúl?...look, I am showing ...
...
*Primary Teacher:* Please, we listen to the person who is speaking. Leandro
　　　　　　is speaking ...
*Infant teacher:* What do you see Leandro?
*Leandro (3):* The line.
*Infant teacher:* Is there one line or many? ...
(Field notes, 21 November 2008. In the Library infant and primary classroom together)

Here the children contribute to the uncovering of knowledge. They take ownership of it and control over its further investigation.

*Infant teacher:* Who painted *La Bañista?*
*Primary teacher:* Joan Miró.
*Infant teacher (to children):* Do you know who is he?
*Teacher :* Ok, ok ... what do you know about Joan Miró?
*Edgar (11):* He is a painter.
*Infant teacher:* In the Library period we can look at his books and we can
　　　　　　read his biography ...
Field notes (21 November 2008. In the Library infant and primary classroom together)

What we want to highlight here is how children can advance their knowledge of writing, reading, vocabulary and calculation from their individual experiences and meanings through the interactions that occur. The teacher studies and interprets the needs and trends revealed by the student. The child knows about himself and can help to develop by self-reference in relation to curriculum guidelines for each of the cycles rather than through competitive comparisons between pupils' performances in standard evaluation procedures and the interactions that take place in the classroom help pupils to advance and become aware of their learning by actively constructing self-sustained and controlled learning processes that make use of a variety of sources of knowledge and inspiration.

The pupils are active subjects in the activities we have followed and through their engagement and production they show themselves to be anything but hopeless learners who are difficult to teach and they also learn and find ways of overcoming the risk of a trauma of school failure for their identity. However, we still have to recognise that regardless of how schools work in terms of their local relationships they are still formally concerned with imposing official knowledge and using the reproduction of this knowledge to reinforce social hierarchies (Bernstein, 2000, 2003) and this means that although using art as a school pedagogy may well accomplish what it set out to do, which is to enhance cultural relevance by restructuring the politics of the classroom to facilitate positive relationships with students, this most likely will not stop these pupils from failing to become identified as successful learners in the long term. But at least it gives them a chance. It might not be social transformation that is encouraged but at least pupils are recognised as creative individuals from industrious and interested families who are worthy of state investment and a meaningful education. They are at least given a chance to become something, to be seen as something and to be able to develop intellectual tools that can be used in school and later life. Creative teaching practices are inclusive practices that emphasise the connection between classroom learning and events outside this setting (Craft and Jeffrey, 2004).

## 5. Discussion: between creativity, performativity and commodification

In this research, the school we have followed offers art as a strategy to accomplish education inclusion through an engagement of emotions and intellects in quite challenging circumstances. We used an ethnographic research process by following teaching practices that used art and documenting and analysing the manner in which children become involved in learning. The concepts of relevance, ownership of knowledge, control of learning processes and innovation on creative schools' projects by Woods and associates were important sensitising concepts in this analysis.

When we analysed the strategies employed by teachers we could see how they perceived the need to promote involvement of the life of students: i.e. relevance; and when our central research questions were what do the main teaching and learning practices in small schools involve and what are the main involvement strategies promoted by these teachers, in terms of the concepts we could see how art was used in the school, to which ends, and how teachers experience the need to facilitate children's involvement through art. We could see that art is present as a way of expression, acceptation and exchange and that free expression is used to articulate the curriculum in a way that connects learning with life and pupil's backgrounds and experiences.

Cooperation in learning rather than competitive learning and assessment were continuous features, promoting a democratic process where children and their personal knowledge, experience and perspectives were recognised and valued. However, in addition, art also offered the possibility of experimenting with alternative orders of representation to produce an impression or to illustrate an association of ideas that pressed beyond surface features. It was a tool for genuinely intellectual work in this sense where empathy and subjectivity were able to become fundamental features in the classroom, in situations where teachers, their pupils and their sensibilities form the key instruments of instruction and learning. Children's emotions and subjectivity were at the centre of their learning. The value of emotion and feeling were recognised and given space in classroom content, as was the incorporation of knowledge from children's social worlds.

But the question still remains as to whether this will be enough to transform these children of a poor, economically exploited transnational migrant labour power in a small village school in a territorially stigmatised economically poor area into successful and positively formally identified *good learners*. Our suspicions from previous research is that they will not and that this will not happen despite the obvious ability of the children in question as learners who are able to reflect, who are motivated, and who can take responsibility not only for their own learning, but also for helping the learning process of their peers and juniors. These pupils also have parents who are interested in their schools and the learning that goes on there. This will quite probably not be enough to overcome social reproduction or challenge education inequity as these things depend distinctly on other social relations well beyond the four walls and two doors of the Lythe school and its library.

There is a clear message communicated by this final recognition. It is that if the pupils do become failures despite their abilities, despite their responsibilities and despite the commitment of their parents and teachers, it is not them nor their culture and background that is the learning problem; as is commonly assumed. It can't be! Instead we suggest it must be *our* culture and the history of dominance of that culture encouraged by an assumed self-superiority of the bourgeois class and the control exercised by members of that class over educational institutions and their curriculum codes, contents, modalities and dominant discourses.

Both Bourdieu and Passeron (1970) and Bernstein (1975, 1990) have expressed similar points to these in other national contexts. Discourses of cultural deficit concerning the people from places such as the one *our school* was located in still persist. Policy mismatch and official representations stubbornly distort real learning problems there. And these features, together with a real material hollowing out of regions and the inability of *markets* to recognise return value possibilities from investments there will most likely continue to create serious problems of educational advancement.

The school as an institution and its teachers are also; along with, as suggested above, the pupils, their backgrounds and their parents; given a large portion of blame for pupil *failure*. However, how truly is this blame apportioned? Our ethnography of art (in) pedagogy at *our school* indicates that the teachers in the school are creative, that they develop curriculum innovations through art as a means to include children in joint learning activities when they might otherwise, through cultural unfamiliarity and language difficulties in Spanish, be excluded, and that pupils and their families respond very positively to this. It also shows that they carry out advanced learning activities in which they make use of school knowledge and outside knowledge as creative subjects who can learn, who are motivated, and who want to learn more. Neither the pupils nor the teachers appear to deserve any blame for negative outcomes in these circumstances. Quite the opposite. The teachers are knowledgeable and conscious professionals who do their utmost to include pupils and encourage their learning and pupils are actively committed to this project.

## 6. Conclusion

This chapter is about learning activities in a small rural school. The school works in line with the creative teaching perspective (Vigo and Soriano, 2014), which emphasises the mediation between classroom learning and events outside this setting. The school offers art as a strategy and we used an ethnographic research process to identify, describe, explain and define teaching practices and how children become involved in learning. The analysis shows how art is present as a way of expression, acceptance and also as a tool of mediation. It shows how pupils learn and that cooperation and learning can be continuous, promoting a democratic process where children are recognised and valued. Art has been a valuable tool in this process. It has offered an arena for experimenting pedagogically with alternative orders of representation in a school that has enabled creative learning to develop and be positively channelled. It has a material foundation and meets a social need. Teachers, pupils and others create spaces of art because they feel they need to in order to maintain educational qualitybecause they feel a genuine value is generated for the school, the community, for its members, including the pupils and their learning. Curriculum planners could possibly learn from this experiment as a means to enable more positive social relations between teachers and pupils, by considering the integration of education through the arts in the formal curriculum. Speculatively what stands in the way of this is the currently dominant position of the symbolic exchange value of schooling and the official content of a predominantly bourgeois curriculum.

## References

Baker, D., (2013) Art integration and cognitive development, *Journal for Learning Through the Arts,* 9(1):17.

Beach, D. and Dovemark, M., (2007) *Education and the commodity problem: Ethnographic investigations of creativity and performativity in Swedish schools*, London: the Tufnell Press.

Bernstein, B., (1975) Class and pedagogies: Visible and invisible, *Educational Studie,s* 1(1):23-41

Bernstein, B., (2000) *Pedagogy, symbolic control and identity: Theory, research and critique*, Maryland: Rowman and Littlefield.

Bernstein, B., (2003) *Class, codes and control. Vol. 4, The structuring of pedagogic discourse*, London: Routledge.

Bernstein, B., (1990) *The structuring of pedagogic discourse*, London: Routledge.

Bourdieu, P. and Passeron, J. C., (1970) *La Reproduction: Éléments pour une théorie du système d'enseignement [Reproduction: Elements for a theory of the educatonal system]*, Paris: Minuit.

Craft, A., (2002) *Creativity and early years education*, London: Continuum.

Craft, A. and Jeffrey, B., (2004) Learner inclusiveness for creative learning, *Education 3-13*, 32(2):39-43.

Cunnington, M., Kantrowitz, A., Harnett, S. and Hill-Ries, A., (2014) Cultivating common ground: Integrating standards-based visual arts, math and literacy in high-poverty urban classrooms, *Journal for Learning through the Arts*, 10(1), Retrieved from https://escholarship.org/uc/item/0377k6x3

Freire, P., (1972/2000) *Pedagogy of the oppressed* (30th anniversary ed.), New York: Continuum.

Hay, S. and Kapitzke, C., (2009) 'Smart state' for a knowledge economy: Reconstituting creativity through student subjectivity, *British Journal of Sociology of Education*, 30(2):151-164.

Hickey-Moody, A. C., (2017) Arts practice as method, urban spaces and intra-active faiths, International *Journal of Inclusive Education*, 21(11):1083-1096.

Jeffrey, B., (2006) Creative teaching and learning: Towards a common discourse and practice, *Journal of Education Policy*, 36(3):399-414.

Jeffrey, B. and Troman, G., (2009) Creative and performativity practices in primary schools: A Foucauldian perspective, *British Educational Research Association Meeting*, 2-5 September, Manchester.

Jeffrey, R., Troman, G. and Phillips, E. Z., (2008) Creative and performativity policies in primary schools, *BERA Annual Conference 2008, September 3-6*, Edinburgh, Heriot-Watt University.

Lundberg, O., (2015) *On cultural racism and school learning: An ethnographic study (Göteborg Studies in Educational Science)*, Göteborg: Acta Universitatis Gothenburgensis.

Troman, G. and Jeffrey, B., (2007) Qualitative data analysis in cross-cultural projects, *Comparative Education*, 43(4):511-525.

Vigo, B. and Soriano, J., (2014) Teaching practices and teachers' perceptions of group creative practices in inclusive rural schools, *Ethnography and Education*, 9(3):253-269.

Woods, P., (1993) *Critical events in teaching and learning*, London: The Falmer Press.

Woods, P. and Jeffrey, B., (1996) *Teachable moments: The art of teaching in primary schools*, Buckingham: Open University Press.

Woods, P. and O' Shannessy, J., (2002) Reintroducing creativity: Day 10 at Hackleton School, *The Curriculum Journal*, 13(2):163-182.

# Chapter 4

## Constructing knowledge in dialogue with rural school children, between art and life

*Giovanna Bacchiddu and Francisco Schwember*

This chapter reports on the unique and unprecedented collaborative ethnographic experience in a small rural school of an interdisciplinary team composed of an anthropologist, author Giovanna Bacchiddu, and an artist/ education Ph.D. candidate, Francisco Schwember. The team was formed within the multidisciplinary Chilean project *Diálogos del Reconocimiento* (Dialogues of Recognition) that started in 2014 as a collaborative endeavour between the School of Art at the Pontificia Universidad Católica de Chile and the Centre for Intercultural and Indigenous Research (CIIR).

The project combined several dyads of anthropologists and accomplished artists. After doing research on specific themes related to Chilean indigenous people, each pair produced a series of artworks and anthropological writings on their chosen topic. The original *Diálogos* project was highly successful, and it was extended for a second edition, which was given the name of *Territorios Alternos* (Alternative Territories). While the second phase of the project maintained the development of research dynamics between pairs of artists and researchers from the social sciences, the novelty of the *Territorios Alternos* project consisted in bringing indigenous communities from different areas of Chile into the collaborative project. Through collaboration, all participants could conceive and co-create new spaces for the production of interdisciplinary knowledge, prompting a dialogue in which Art and the Social Sciences converge in indigenous settings, with the aim of 'generating a place of creation and reflection on intercultural relations: an artistic exhibition that produces knowledge through the construction of visual works that elicit anthropological, sociological and historical reflections. These have as a thematic axis the failed recognition of the multicultural identity of Chile' (http://dialogosdelreconocimiento.cl)

This project fulfilled the need to integrate the claims of Chile's indigenous peoples into national public debates, along with recognition of the country's contested multicultural identity. The artists produced works of art based on the research, which was driven by the ethnographic approach and the fruitful interaction and collaboration with the community and the anthropologist. Due to the long-term research experience and familiarity of the anthropologist with the field site Apiao— a small, rural island in southern Chile, with a population of approximately 700 inhabitants of indigenous origin—was included in the *Territorios Alternos* project. Within the island, the setting of choice was one of the two rural schools, which is currently attended by thirty schoolchildren who range in age from four to twelve years old. After a preliminary research and preparation phase, the anthropologist and the artist/educator travelled to the island to spend a week at the school, taking part in the daily activities with the schoolchildren and their teachers, sharing with them time, space, and conversations, and engaging with them in several artistic activities and creative practices.

The Apiao setting and its project were chosen from among several to be the subject of a short documentary film. The team was thus joined by filmmaker Josefina Buschmann who, together with a sound technician, filmed and recorded the school activities prompted by the artist and anthropologist. This chapter reports ethnographic findings from this collaborative, multidisciplinary experience from both the anthropologist's point of view, formed after fifteen years of research, and the artist/educator, who contributed his expertise and unique perspective on the data.

## 1. The setting: The island of Apiao

The setting for our research and art project, Apiao, is a small rural island belonging to the archipelago of Chiloé in southern Chile. Apiao's residents practice agriculture, small animal farming, and algae and shellfish collecting. The island currently hosts a basic medical post, two schools, and a nursery. Nowadays the local children can attend school on the island from the age of four years-old to fifteen years-old. If they want to attend college, they can do so by moving to the nearest small town, Achao, which is approximately two to three hours away by boat. Achao is the island's reference point for shopping, bureaucracy, higher education, and medical attention, with islanders travelling there regularly. Unlike other islands of Chiloé, most of Apiao's inhabitants are of indigenous origin; their indigeneity, coupled with their rural lifestyle and their geographical marginality, has implied enduring stereotypical labelling and a triple stigma (Grenier, 1984). In Chile people born and raised on the islands—especially those distant from the *modern* towns—are generally considered backward, ignorant, attached to superstition, or otherwise incompatible with *modernity*. Apiao people have indeed felt neglected by the state and disconnected from the rest of the country for a long time, due to the lack of access to central electricity and running water. These services have been provided by the Chilean state only very recently (see Bacchiddu, 2017).

Most locals in Apiao are Catholics and their religious affiliation implies active participation in a network of alliances between neighbours and relatives. One of the most important values on the island is reciprocity, which is honoured on a regular basis as well as on the occasion of events connected to the agricultural cycle, important religious celebrations, and unique life events. Most celebrations and pivotal events happen in the household, the physical space comprising the house, where people live, eat and sleep, and the fields, where people cultivate their crops and attend to their domestic animals. All members of the household participate actively in these occasions, as well as in the typical daily routine, where everyone has multiple tasks to accomplish.

## 2. Apiao children: An ethnographic look

Apiao children are active members of their household from an early age. They are immersed in the daily routine from the time they are toddlers and learn basic tasks from their parents, grandparents or elder siblings. Children continuously receive important social knowledge while in the household, and from an early age they learn the proper ways to reply to the elders, attend to guests, address people, offer food and drinks, and be polite. They learn the boundaries between individuals and know what is expected of them. They are eager to help in household tasks because they know that the adults will appreciate them as long as they are able to perform those tasks. They learn from an early age to act like adults and indeed, they can seem like little adults. They achieve this by carefully listening to what the adults of the household say and observing attentively what they do, rarely asking questions or seeking explanations. Rather, they reproduce the words, gestures and postures they observe regularly. This is not an imitation or a passive reproduction, but is always a complex and creative interpretation of a code of conduct that has been internalised.

Apiao children spend considerable amounts of time in the fields nearby the household and at the beach, immersed in the natural surroundings where their parents work. They usually accompany the adults in the daily tasks, and have the opportunity to observe and learn the proper way to act, starting from simple skills to more elaborate ones. They continuously practice the knowledge of the environment, by engaging with it: playing, walking and running in it, using it, and experimenting with it. Children explore nature, its living beings—plants and animals—and accumulate natural knowledge together with social knowledge at one and the same time. They are generally obedient, respectful, and silent, eagerly waiting to be given some task by a family member. In the presence of guests or other adults, or when visiting other households, they are generally shy and remain silent, acting politely. Acting politely in this case entails remaining silent, but this implies neither discomfort nor submission: being polite is considered the appropriate way to act for a child, and a polite child is greatly appreciated and praised in public, as is a child who performs chores in the household. Children learn from an early age to be responsible, skilled, and independent; they will accept small responsibilities and take care of *their* tasks daily, which will increase with time.

The adults are the children's main interlocutors, however, learning occurs mostly by silent observation, being articulated through sharing time together and having the children perform small tasks that are learned by observing and acquiring familiarity with them. This type of informal learning is found in many Amerindian cultures, and has been described by several authors, who have declared it a phenomenon worthy of academic analysis, and have isolated specific elements that characterise it. Amongst these are the social organisation of the learning process, the role of the expert, the difference aspects of observation, the facets of motivation, the presence of initiative, the use of language, and the use of non-verbal communication (Paradise, 2005).

Gaskins and Paradise (2010) aptly pointed out how this kind of learning, called observational learning, is enmeshed in everyday interaction and is often invisible, or unmarked. This closely reflects what happens in Apiao, although it cannot be argued, as these authors do, that the children are 'expected to always be observing and to keep their attention in the here and now' (Gaskins and Paradise, 2010: 100): the children are inserted in the adults' world, while the adults do not pay too much attention to them, nor do they encourage them to observe or be alert—this just happens spontaneously. As a result, they are fairly independent and completely at ease with their environment. In Apiao the instructions given to children are little and very specific, mostly aimed at prompting them to do something—a specific action (Paradise, 1991).

In this culture there is little verbal interaction, and a child is hardly ever seen asking her parents a question or an explanation regarding what to do or how to do it. Being skilled in a range of practical, domestic tasks earns the child respect and social acceptance and recognition; it means admission into the world of the adults, an admission eagerly desired amongst Apiao children just like amongst the Mazahua ones described by Paradise (2005); see also the concept of *pitching in* developed by Paradise and Rogoff (2009).

## 3. Apiao children in school: The constraints of formal education

If growing up in an Apiao household and the land that surrounds it allows children to develop a strong sense of independence and self-reliance, going to school represents a dramatic change for them. Formal education highlights the profound difference between the family world and the institutionalised world of the school. The children must follow instructions, take orders regarding the use of their bodies, wear uniforms, adopt a specific physical posture, and adhere to a discipline. They are constantly given a series of directives and tasks by adult teachers who are not their parents, and who always tell them exactly what to do. The tasks are generally new and unfamiliar, and not very attractive—the children cannot relate them to anything they have experience of in the real world. As a result, they are often disoriented, confused or sometimes at a complete loss, which can result in them being left behind. Their learning pace is generally slow, and teachers often face unresponsive or indifferent children who passively plod through a seemingly insurmountable task. As Lancy (2015: 1033) observes, such reactions would be labelled *a disorder* in the US and generally in the industrial Western world.

Undoubtedly, there is a fracture between the two modes of knowledge transmission, socialisation and learning that underlines the distance between the familiar/traditional and the unknown/institutional. This same phenomenon of discontinuity between home and school, informal and institutionalised learning has been observed by several anthropologists working in rural and traditional communities in Amerindian societies and beyond (e.g. Spindler, 2000; Paradise and Rogoff, 2009; Szulc, 2013). Lancy (2015) calls it *a mismatch*, after revising several anthropological studies of successful transmission of knowledge through informal learning, which inevitably clash with the system when confronted with formal schooling. Paradise (2005, and in most of her work) points out that schools inevitably promote a loss of autonomy in the children, with their emphasis on projection towards the future, while the children are used to focus on an immediate satisfaction borne out of an action with instant, practical results, the ability to getting things done, now.

According to the observation conducted in Apiao, removing children from their everyday household routine and placing them in a somewhat artificial environment originates confusion. The most obvious consequence of this is low academic performance. In this geographical area, however, low academic performance is only part of the problem: the Chiloé region presents an extremely elevated percentage (nearing fifty per cent) of students who are diagnosed with varying degrees of learning disabilities (*Plan Anual de Desarrollo Educativo Municipal 2018*, Corporación Municipal de Quinchao). Unsurprisingly, these children have no problems performing the practical tasks that they undertake daily at home.

In the small rural school there are only three classrooms: one for kindergarten children, one for first through third-year children, and one for the older children from fourth-year to sixth-year. In total, there are thirty children. Only three of the handful of teachers are locals, and most teachers are in their twenties or early thirties. In line with Paradise's findings, observing the children in the classroom, what was mostly evident was their lack of autonomy and profound insecurity. They appeared needy, constantly requiring the teacher's full attention: i.e. '*Tío, ¿qué hago? Tía, ¿cómo se hace?*' (Sir, what do I do? Madam, how do I do this?). They continuously asked for explanations and waited for the teacher's evaluation of the little task they recently performed, and when they failed to obtain it, they played, got up, or did nothing. They were easily distracted, and their attention span was very low; they frequently got up and checked what their classmates were doing, or queued to ask further instructions of the teacher, who passed from pupil to pupil, endlessly repeating tasks and explanations. The whole impression was one of restlessness and chaos. This was the general atmosphere that characterised the classroom, especially among the younger pupils.

When I asked the teachers to comment on the apparent discrepancy between how they are extremely independent at home, and inversely, how they appear fully dependent on teachers' instructions and feedback before taking any action at school, one of them said:

> Some of them are not very proactive; you have to tell them what to do. But they do it! For them being independent at home is natural. They see what the adults do, they know exactly what they have to do because they observe every action of the adults, and they know. This is what is missing here, that they get to the point where they can do it naturally just like they do it at home.

During our workshops, we increasingly managed to captivate the children's attention, thanks to the novelty of our presence, the tasks required, and the material used. This is evidenced in that they felt free to create and to imagine, with their artistic production during our interventions, even if undoubtedly their classroom attitude of dependency and general lack of initiative emerged most of the time.

Figure 4.1: Apiao Municipal School—Art workshop with Francisco Schwember. Chiloé (Chile), 2016

This pattern changed abruptly, though, once we took the classroom outside. We decided to involve them in an effort to recover the knowledge of their ancestors, for which they had to leave the school premises and work outdoors. We organised a workshop on dyeing wool with plants and flowers, recreating an activity that used to be regularly practiced until the recent past by the elder inhabitants of the island. To achieve thist, we carried out research with some of the pupils' grandparents on the natural fibres that were commonly used and on the practical process of dyeing. We then invited the entire population of children to join us for a walking trip to the countryside, where we asked them to collect the material we needed, allowing them to roam free in the fields and show us the way.

We took a chance to get to the beach, where we instructed the children to collect and gather the abundant litter found locally, with the idea of building a work of art made with plastic and other rubbish that contaminates the Chiloé coastline. We could detect a profound change in the children during our outdoor expedition, which implied walking in the open air and interacting with nature both in the fields and at the beach. The children recovered their usual personality, freedom, confidence, and autonomy and this was evident in their body posture, facial expressions, and general attitude with respect to the space and place. Following Paradise (1991: 77), the children recovered a specific interactional medium that promotes both the children' expression and their autonomy, allowing them to take the initiative. They were at ease with the environment and they could show it to us proudly. Drawing on Morelli's work (2013) it could be argued that these outdoor activities allowed the multi-sensorial engagement that is so often missing in the formal educational curriculum, and that is at the root of learning for these children. Accomplishing tasks in the open air meant for the children a reconnection with some of their habitual (and favourite) activities, which are 'sensorially rewarding' (Morelli, 2013: 62) and stimulate the affective engagement of the children with the environment.

Figure 4.2: Walking trip with the schoolchildren. Apiao, Chiloé (Chile), 2016

This is how one of the teachers put it: "They have an intimate relationship with nature and with their natural surroundings; they are one with nature". It was indeed surprising to see for ourselves the depth of the knowledge they have, and display, with respect to their environment. While outdoors, they also showed a different attitude towards each other: they were caring of one another and they were protective toward us during our trip. They looked after us while we jumped fences, crossed wooden railings, and went through paths covered in thorny bushes. Pablo (pseudonym), a third-year boy, waited purposely for everyone to pass by because he wanted to be the last person of the group, so that by being behind he could enjoy a panoramic view of the whole group and could take care of any problems that might arise. "I know this place very well!" he kept saying with a wide smile.

## 4. The interdisciplinary project in the Chiloé context

When the *Territorios Alternos* project began, we knew that taking part in it implied not only being receptive to new settings and experiences, but also re-interpreting the scope of our professional training. Through this project, the traditional boundaries of our individual trajectories as a visual artist in the process of completing a Ph.D. in education and an anthropologist were reconsidered, in order to contribute our expertise to a collective interdisciplinary endeavour. Furthermore, we had the opportunity to benefit from the collaboration of audio-visual artist Josefina Buschmann who filmed and recorded the activities that were carried out in the school in order to produce a documentary film.

The geographical and cultural context of the island of Apiao made the challenge presented by the project even more palpable. We were facing an unprecedented collective work on a remote corner of the archipelago of Chiloé, whose unique characteristics result from a process of colonisation anchored in a cultural context that is historically marked by isolation and marginality from the rest of the national territory. In the culture of Chiloé spaces of syncretism emerged from the confluence of native peoples like the Huilliches and the Chonos with the Spanish conquerors; the unique cultural landscape that emerges is also due to the occupation of a geographic/cultural area that has been aptly named *maritorio*, given the historical preponderance of the maritime life and the occupation of the border over the interior valleys of this archipelago.

This Chiloé culture was able to develop creative and distinctive solutions in diverse spheres of knowledge, from the elaboration of artifacts to solve different needs of everyday life, to the complexity achieved in naval and architectural construction using wood. Some notable examples include the churches declared World Heritage by UNESCO, which emerged from the work developed jointly by the Jesuit order and Chiloé communities in what was called the Circular Mission.[1]

The chosen setting was one of the island's rural schools. This particular context presented a privileged space to reflect on various issues that are fundamental

---

1.  The Circular Mission was a system of annual evangelisation trips carried out by the Jesuits in the Chiloé archipelago from the seventeenth century until the expulsion of the order in 1767, to be later continued by the Franciscan order (Urbina, 1983).

to our disciplines. Particularly so in Francisco's case, being an artist who has developed research and creative projects that address the relationship between art, education and knowledge.

## 5. The art project's goals and methodology

How could our disciplinary perspectives of art and anthropology help us approach the relationship between the particular knowledge of the place and a contemporary artistic project? What continuities or discontinuities could we find between life and school for the island's children we interacted with? These were some of the questions we had in mind when we travelled to the island, alert to the privilege to open up receptively to the community and their ways of life.

Sharing time, space, and knowledge with the community and its culture implied that this relationship and exchange would be reflected in Francisco's work as an artist, and would inform it. He was open to receiving local forms of knowledge and, through the strategies and methodologies coming from the visual arts, he wished to generate a new space for the creation of knowledge, both for us researchers and for the communities involved.

We conducted interviews with various members of the school community (students, teachers, and family members), in order to learn their views on their school's aesthetic environment, the entirety of sensorial aspects that participate in the constitution of the school space (interior and exterior spaces of the building, materials, odours, colours, construction, green areas, images, etc.), and to understand their opinion and needs concerning the institution, particularly with regard to the school's physical premises. At the same time, we developed and ran intensive art workshops focused on school children with the aim of manufacturing various visual products (drawings, paintings, clay models, and similar) inspired by the island's history. These workshops implied having the children to reflect on and talk about their past, as well as their natural and cultural environment.

This approach resulted in the children being confronted in the classroom with materials traditionally used in the school's art curriculum, reproducing standardised and uniform responses to the issues raised. The invitation to think creatively about their spatial and cultural context through artistic forms obtained a response that could have been elaborated by children anywhere in the country. What was striking was that while doing the tasks we gave them, the children constantly required our validation and approval, as if there were a correct solution to the invitation to create freely. As mentioned above, we strongly felt the children's insecurity and distress in the face of assignments for which they did not feel prepared. Although we developed various strategies to encourage them to respond with greater ease and confidence, we did not obtain better results. This first evaluation yielded several questions, above all referring to the contrast between the richness, originality, and versatility of the Chiloé culture and the doubtful and timid character shown by the students inside the classroom. The anthropological literature review on themes related to education and learning undoubtedly helped us to put this apparent contradiction into an Amerindian, and a more global, context.

## 6. Recovering fragments of knowledge and engaging with the environment

During our stay at the home of two elderly residents of the island, we prompted a conversation on their lifestyle and daily routine before the rapid modernisation process that this area experienced over the last two decades. Within a permanent context of isolation and self-sufficiency, the inhabitants of the island had to provide their own food, manufacture their houses and boats, and produce many of their own clothes and utensils. Delving deeper into this last aspect, we could listen to the elderly couple reminiscing about the process of dyeing the most commonly used natural fibre, sheep wool, that was habitually coloured with natural dyes that were obtained locally, applying ancestral knowledge of the native flora.

After learning from the elders the characteristics of each plant, along with the basics of the dyeing process, we proposed to the school community the idea of embarking on a journey to recover that knowledge. This somewhat unexpected development meant we had to modify our work plan, leaving the school premises to go outside all together, as a group. Letting the children wander out and explore the rich natural space that surrounds the establishment, giving them a chance to re-discover it and to show it to us, was a particularly fruitful experiment. The group expedition dynamic replaced, and reversed, the traditional teacher-student role that defines school interactions. This strategy promoted an alternative process of teaching and learning that emphasised horizontality and fluidity among participants; it also gave the children the opportunity to guide the process and actively express and display their relations with the environment.

It is worth mentioning that the natural environment that surrounds the school is characterised by the omnipresence of the sea and wind, as well as the land, remnants of native forests, and grasslands transformed into cultivated fields by the families of the children. These surroundings are populated by different species of domestic and wild animals, especially birds, that provide a constant and intense soundscape. The atmosphere is in a permanent, and spectacular, change of light and colour.

Once out of the classroom and into the open space, the children displayed a surprising change of attitude. They began to behave with the autonomy and competence with which they habitually perform in their daily lives; they exhibited a free, proactive, and playful spirit that recalls the most innovative experiences of the *Forest Schools* and offers another interpretation to Maturana and Varela's (1984: 116) aphorism, *living is knowing*, where the subject knows through sensorial experience that is associated with a strong connection with the environment.

This new dynamic allowed Francisco to adjust his role as a teacher, a figure conventionally understood as carrying and transmitting validated knowledge that is, in turn, received and absorbed by the student community through the teaching and learning process. Instead, he became a facilitator in the rediscovery of fragments of traditional knowledge that appeared to be in the process of being forgotten. Furthermore, his role as an artist and teacher was enriched by the integration of ethnographic strategies and resources. These emerged in the collaboration with Giovanna, together with the fundamental contribution of her knowledge and experience of the island gathered over more than fifteen years. This allowed us to articulate a consistent and critical look at the social phenomena we approached, with an ethnographic view characteristic of the contemporary art world (Foster, 2001).

In this way, Francisco's role as a teacher was transformed into one that required assuming, in part, the logic of 'learning to unlearn in order to re-learn' (Mignolo, 2010: 98), which led to a relationship of circularity with the community, in a sort of loop. First, he had to learn pieces of knowledge from community members that were in a rapid process of loss; then he had to become a transmitter of that knowledge to the new generations. Remarkably, the school does not currently represent a space of recognition and recovery of this collective knowledge.

## 7. Some observations on the project from the visual arts field

For Francisco this experience resulted in a long process of reflection about his two main areas of interest (art and education), leading to several conclusions. In the first place, he questioned the established borders that separate notions of contemporary art from indigenous and popular art. In this context, he saw the evidence of the limited dimension of art defined from a eurocentric vision, which prioritises the disciplinary knowledge coming from the West over other knowledge anchored in the traditional ways of life found in indigenous communities, with the devaluation and invisibilisation this entails.

It also became apparent that the school faces difficulty in receiving and transmitting valuable traditional knowledge, which fuses and dilutes boundaries between crafts, design, architecture, and art. The pedagogical potential offered by the recovery of traditional knowledge became clear; the evidence showed how it allows greater continuity in the relationship between school and daily life. In this area, the recognition of other ways of creating knowledge, say with contributions by *mestizo*[2] people, or people of humble origins, are particularly relevant, as they allow us to visualise other possible interpretations of artistic creation and education in the Latin American context (Escobar, 2008).

As an example, in the case of the island of Apiao, the collective practices used in the construction, maintenance, and preservation of various apparatuses and structures of daily use on the island go beyond any training found within formal education. Rather, they deploy a multiplicity of creative resources anchored in informal practices, based both in the ancestral traditions inherited from indigenous canoeists, for instance, and in the skills of sailors, carpenters, and farmers who produced a series of solutions typical of a precarious and, until very recently, autarkic environment. It is extremely common to find throughout the island rudimentary boats made with recycled waste from the salmon industry, as well as ingenious door locks carved from native wood, not to mention the local construction of boats and buildings. This local knowledge has been directly applied in the well-known ecclesiastical architecture that brought Chiloé to global fame.

Furthermore, through his role as a teacher, Francisco was able to open a small space for the articulation of what Ilich has called a *learning community* (Ilich, 2012), which highlights the pre-Columbian tradition of the *minga*, where

2. a term traditionally used in Spain, Latin America and the Philippines that originally referred to a person of combined European and Native American descent, regardless of where the person was born. Particularly in Latin America, mestizo has become more of a cultural term, with culturally mainstream Latin Americans regarded or termed as mestizos regardless of their actual ancestry and with the term Indian being reserved exclusively for people who have maintained a separate indigenous ethnic identity, language, tribal affiliation, and similar cultural attributes. Consequently, today, the vast majority of Spanish-speaking Latin Americans are regarded as Mestizos. Wikipedia.

collective and free work is offered for the common good, always according to a principle of reciprocity. This constitutes a collective construction of meaning, where the teacher-disciple relationship is blurred and becomes a cooperative relationship, whose potentiality has not been fully exploited by the country's school system.

The work our team carried out has implied taking a political approach with diverse facets, not only because of our involvement with a doubly marginalised community—due to its geographical location and its ethnic origin (Grenier, 1984), but also because of our firm will to develop intercultural and interdisciplinary work that seeks to open spaces for what has been called *epistemic disobedience* (Mignolo, 2010). This concept was meant as a critique to the eurocentric framework that regulates the production of knowledge at the academic level, and the subordinate role assigned to indigenous people and other marginalised communities in the production of knowledge in disciplines such as art.

Parallel to the process developed on the island, epistemological questions were formulated in a very specific way in the elaboration of the visual work that was to be exhibited as part of the project in various artistic spaces in the country. The visual work gradually integrated materials and construction procedures typical of the culture of the region of Chiloé. This process, guided by arts-based research (Sullivan, 2005; Borgdorff, 2010; Finley and Knowles, 1995), allows for a broadening of theoretical perspectives and assigns a preponderant role to the process of creation and research that extends beyond the scope of traditional research in social sciences by integrating processes and methodologies of the arts in the creation of new knowledge. Furthermore, it gives special relevance to relationships of cooperation established between the researcher and the communities that participate in the research.

In this way, Francisco elaborated a series of visual works that recovered different aspects of the life of the community of the island of Apiao. They arose from various areas of interest discovered on the island, highlighting the close existential connection of its inhabitants with their natural environment, where the experience of sailing, the constant presence of the native forest, the ever-changing light, the wind, the birds, and the dolphins, are overwhelming. The native forest is visualised in the traditional wooden construction of houses and churches, as well as in the religious imagery that enriches them. The obvious consequences of time become patent as this modifies and alters the various woods. These wooden constructions are of uncommon dimensions within

Western architecture; the smell of the native wood offers an olfactory dimension that makes the forest breathe through architecture.

Figure 4.3: Class Lessons Exhibition—Museo de la Educación Gabriela Mistral. Santiago de Chile, 2017

Likewise, the re-evaluation of the indigenous roots of the community made it possible to approach the elaboration of visual work as a space for an encounter with their past and their relationship with nature. In this context, the piece of art called *El espacio anterior* (The Previous Space), representing foliage, made of handmade blue paper, and populated by golden stars, refers not only to the traditional iconography of Chiloé church vaults, but also recovers the celestial vault as a permanent space of nomadic habitation, giving a nod to the primordial blue in indigenous cosmology, the origin of the first man (Chihuailaf, 1999). At the same time, the work integrates metaphorically the relationship between knowledge and nature, through the incorporation of a school desk whose legs turn into tree branches/roots that tie together life with learning.

## 8. Some considerations on discontinuities and recovery

Our joint experience of intervention in the rural school of the island of Apiao, Chiloé, allowed both of us—artist and anthropologist—to enjoy a privileged view of a social and cultural minority that is fundamentally marginal to the Chilean national social, economic, and cultural world. While interacting with a small group of children of indigenous origin who have spent all their life in a small, rural, and isolated place, immersed in nature, we realised how the national school programs are severely limited in their attempt to protect and valorise local cultural traits. Priority is given to the national requirements, which tend to treat all schools as if they were a homogeneous whole, without taking into account the cultural and geographic specificities of each area. As a result, chunks of local knowledge are being rapidly forgotten, especially now that the islanders have access to some aspects of modernity, such as electricity and running water, which have been denied to them for a long time (see Bacchiddu, 2017). One of the teachers, a local, told us:

> Things have changed since when I was in school here. We used to do several workshops, we learned craftwork—to produce with natural elements such as the local wool, or with stuff we used to find at the beach—we used to spend more time outside in the open air. Now things have changed because schools are required to produce different kinds of knowledge, and artisanal skills are not included in the standard national requirements. We have to show how our school is well versed in sports and gymnastic or musical education, and we participate in regional competitions with other schools. There's no space anymore for workshops on arts and crafts, or recycling. And this is what is missing; but it's not just us, it's at the national level because we have to abide by the rules.

Our experience in Apiao can be summarised as an experience of discontinuity, and of recovery. During our project, we dealt with several discontinuities that emerged powerfully. Some of these are tradition and modernity; life at home and life at school; local knowledge and formal training; traditional lore and artistic project; anthropology and art.

This insular community keeps firmly rooted in tradition for what concerns its religious beliefs, social values, as well as traditional forms of social relations and ways of forming alliances, that occur following a strict unwritten code and almost sacred etiquette (Bacchiddu, 2012). At the same time, the powerful call of modernity has settled amongst the islanders, who do not want to be cut off from the modern market, and are willing to be protagonists rather than spectators in a modern, fast-changing world (Bacchiddu, 2017). We have pointed out throughout this chapter how the way to transmit knowledge in the household and in communitarian contexts clashes with formal institutional learning; the children suffer from this mismatch and pay the price of this powerful discontinuity that affects their emotional life as well as their academic performance (Lancy, 2015; Spindler, 2000).

The traditional artisanal production has the primary objective of being useful; each object is conceived for practical use and applications, and no local would see artistic value in it. And yet, the trained artist sees how the local knowledge is fully retrievable and how its multifaceted aspects can be recovered and applied in the creation of ethnographically informed, contemporary art pieces.

Finally, combining art and anthropology in an innovative project implied an interesting challenge for us, both accustomed to be confined to our disciplines with a form of exclusivity justified by our respective academic responsibilities.

The *Territorios Alternos* multidisciplinary project was itself an (perhaps discrepant) attempt to resolve some of these discrepancies, allowing two different forms of expertise and sensibilities to collaborate, communicate, and exchange knowledge between themselves, in dialogue with the school children. One of the tools that allowed us to successfully progress has been the strategy, and long-term goal, of recovery. Through the dyeing workshop, certain forms of lost and forgotten knowledge were recovered and applied by the children to produce several batches of colourful, and completely natural, sheep wool. Together with the recovery of intangible heritage, the project produced the recovery of significant local material: the Apiao church committee donated a batch of wooden *alerce* tiles (*Fitzroya cupressoides* tree, currently a protected species) to Francisco, so that he could recycle them and include them in his work of art. The tiles used to belong to the original nineteenth-century roof of the island's church. The roof was renovated about a decade ago and substituted with corrugated iron material. *Alerce* tiles used to be ubiquitous; they are now extremely expensive and people tend to build their homes with other material that is cheaper and more readily available. The old buildings, entirely made with *alerce*, are usually dismantled and the tiles are destined to be burned in the stove, which in Chiloé is constantly running.

The old, beautiful, and precious *alerce* tiles were sitting at the back of the church, ready to be burned when needed, for a patron saint *fiesta* or another religious occasion. They were assembled by Francisco and now constitute his work *La rosa de los muertos* (The Rose of the Dead): the *alerce* façades intend to account for the rich patrimonial heritage of Chiloé, and at the same time, when converted into the shape of a wind rose on the floor, they convey the maritime character of this culture while highlighting the living and constant presence of nature.

The process of creating such visual work, with direct references to the maritime culture of the Chiloé archipelago, constitutes a central element in the process of research-creation developed within the framework of this project. *Territorios Alternos* allowed us to integrate knowledge originated and managed by the community itself; at the same time, the community was no longer simply a group being studied but became an active part of the process of research and creation.

## Acknowledgement

The authors gratefully acknowledge the CIIR for financing the *Diálogos del Reconocimiento* project; the staff at the Escuela Rural Metahue of Apiao for hosting us, and the generous Apiao families for providing accommodation, food and company during our stay. The project was designed by author Francisco Schwember as an artist and co-curator, together with the artist and researcher Danilo Espinoza.

## References

Borgdorff, H., (2010) The production of knowledge in artistic research, in Biggs, M. and Karlsson. H., (eds.), *The research companion to research in the arts*, Oxon, UK: Routledge.

Bacchiddu, G., (2012) 'Doing things properly': Religious aspects in everyday sociality in Apiao, Chiloé, in Skielke, S. and Debevec, L. (eds.), *Ordinary lives and grand schemes: An anthropology of everyday religion*, Oxford: Berghahn.

Bacchiddu, G., (2017) Updating the map of desires: Mobile phones, satellite dishes and abundance as facets of modernity in Apiao, Chiloé, Southern Chile, *Suomen Antropologi: Journal of the Finnish Anthropological Society*, 42(1):45-66.

Carlson, A. and Berleant, A., (2004) *The aesthetics of natural environments*, Ontario: Broadview Press.

Chihuailaf, E., (1999) *Recado confidencial a los chilenos [A confidential chore to Chileans]*, Santiago de Chile: LOM.

Escobar, T., (2008) *El mito del arte y el mito del pueblo: Cuestiones sobre arte popular [The myth of art and the myth of the people: Questions about popular art]*, Santiago de Chile: Metales pesados.

Finley, S., and Knowles, J. G., (1995) Researcher as artist/artist as researcher, *Qualitative Inquiry* 1(1):110-142.

Foster, H., (2001) *El retorno de lo real: La Vanguardia a finales de siglo [The return of the real: Vanguardism at the end of the century]*, Madrid: Akal.

Gaskins, S. and Paradise, R., (2010) Learning through observation in daily life, in Lancy, D., Bock, J. and Gaskins, S., (eds.) *The anthropology of learning in childhood*, Plymouth, UK: AltaMira Press.

Grenier, P., (1984) *Chiloé et les Chilotes: marginalité et dépendence en Patagonie chilienne: Étude de geographie humaine [Chiloé and the Chilotes: marginality and dependence in Chilean Patagonia]*, Aix-en-Provence: EDISUD.

Ilich, I., (2012) *La sociedad desescolarizada [Deschooling society]*, Buenos Aires: Godot.

Lancy, D.F., (2015) *The anthropology of childhood: Cherubs, chattel, changelings*, Cambridge: Cambridge University Press.

Maturana, H. and Varela, F.J., (1984) *El árbol del conocimiento: Las bases biológicas del entendimiento humano [The tree of knowledge: Biological basis of human understanding]*, Santiago de Chile: Lumen.

Mignolo, W., (2010) *Desobediencia epistémica: Retórica de la modernidad, lógica de la colonialidad y gramática de la decolonialidad [Epistemic disobedience: Rhetoric of modernity, the logic of colonialism and the grammar of decolonialism]*, Buenos Aires: Del Signo.

Morelli, C., (2013) Teaching in the rainforest: Exploring Matses children's affective engagement and multisensory experiences in the classroom environment, *Teaching Anthropology*, 2(2):53-65.

Paradise, R., (1991) El conocimiento cultural en el aula: Niños indígenas y su orientación hacia la observación [Cultural knowledge in the classroom: Indigenous children and their orientation towards observation], *Infancia y Aprendizaje*, 55:73-85.

Paradise, R., (2005) Motivación e iniciativa en el aprendizaje informal [Motivation and initiative in informal learning], *Revista Electronica Sinectica*, 26:12-21.

Paradise, R. and Rogoff, B., (2009) Side by side: Learning by observing and pitching in, *Ethnos*, 37(1):102-138.

Spindler, G. and Spindler, L., (2000) *Fifty years of anthropology and education, 1950-2000: A Spindler anthology*, New York: Psychology Press.

Sullivan, G., (2005) *Art practice as research: Inquiry in the visual arts*, London: Sage.

Szulc, A., (2013) 'Eso me enseñé con los chicos': Aprendizaje entre pares y contextualizado entre niños mapuche del Neuquén ['That's what I taught myself with the kids': Peer and contextualized learning between Mapuche children in the Neuquén], *Boletín de Antropología y Educación*, 4(6):37-43.

Urbina B., (1983) *La periferia meridional indiana: Chiloé en el siglo XVIII [The meridional indigenous periphery: Chiloé in the XVIIth century]*, Valparaiso: Ediciones Universitarias de Valparaiso.

**Chapter 5**

# Misrecognitions in the practice of art and ethnography

*Andrew Hewitt and Mel Jordan*

## 1. Introduction

In his 1995 essay *Artist as ethnographer?*, Hal Foster asks a particularly pertinent question, 'What misrecognitions have passed between anthropology and art and other discourses?' (Foster, 1995: 302). Some of the misrecognitions that occur between art and other discourses are related to the contingent nature of art; the way in which art is recounted by artists, historians and theorists, through the ontological question, 'what is art?' which subsequently takes us to the question, 'what can art be?' The debates that ensue expose the extent of art's internal rivalries and demonstrates the contested nature of art. Gabriel Rockhill, in his book *Radical history and the politics of art* (Rockhill, 2014) describes the danger of engaging in ontological descriptive questions. Admittedly here, he compares art and politics, but the method he describes might help us appreciate the problem. He asserts that the nature of art and politics are not essential, as there are very many competing articulations from numerous positions and methodological perspectives appertaining to both art and politics. Therefore, there is little use in engaging in ontological descriptive questions, thus trying to answer the query, 'what is art?' or, 'what is politics?' (Rockhill, 2014: 219) does not get us anywhere; the result is an exhaustive list of all the things that it might be, could be, has said to be, and so on. Nevertheless, we discover, through our investigation of recent art and social science projects, that a more thorough understanding of the complexity of art (and sociology) is necessary in order to maximise its political potential for social intervention.

Although Foster first posed this problem in 1995 it remains an on-going consideration for those engaged in producing social and political artworks. Today the implication of this question has gained in relevance due to the way in which art is commissioned and produced through global biennales, culture-led regeneration projects, as well as gallery education and outreach programmes in the public realm. Under New Labour, for example, art was put to work to meet the policy agendas of health, social cohesion and urban development, this use of art to help improve other government activity enabled funding to become available for social art based-projects (Hewitt, 2011: 23).

Foster outlines the specific assumptions that have emerged for art and its arrangement with anthropology; in short, art addresses the historical problematic of anthropology, that of regarding the anthropologist as the objective observer. However, this contested norm is turned on its head and the result is that it is only acceptable for those who have been historically observed, affected by, and colonised by powerful others who can comment on those injustices within contemporary culture. Within this assembly there is a supposition that artistic transformation is the same 'site of political transformation' (Foster, 1995: 302) and that this transformation occurs elsewhere, in the 'field of the other', what Foster (1995: 302) describes as 'the oppressed postcolonial, subaltern, or subcultural'. This presents us with a problem as this alterity, this *outsider-ness* is identified as the key technique towards a political critique of a dominant culture; so, if the artist is not the exploited proletariat or the oppressed post-colonial subaltern then she cannot legitimately speak to or represent these ideas. And, conversely if she is, she has an automatic right to do so. Foster is troubled by the result of this configuration—applying an ethic to representation does not resolve the issue of not speaking for another, rather it gives us an equivalent political problem—one of not *being able to speak for* another.

## 2. Social artist as sensory ethnographer

Contemporary art likes anthropology because it engages with similar models of assembly; process, content and context being key to both disciplines. And like art, anthropology brings with it an internal critique, one of social responsibility, namely objectivity. So, while a contemporary artist asks, 'who am I to assert my autonomy over this social situation?', the anthropologist longs to be objective.

Nevertheless, Foster reasons that ultimately art cannot address the same social codes of anthropology because the two activities have different relations of production. Although, *quasi-anthropological* (Foster, 1995: 303)—artists utilise methods akin to those used by ethnographers—they cannot do so without allowing for the histories, theories and practices of art itself. In the most part, art returns to its familiar social relations; the artwork, the exhibition, the viewer, the commissioner, the curator, the collector and so on. Evidently anthropology does produce cultural and political capital, but the value that it generates operates differently as it does not produce objects for economic exchange.

Moreover, for Foster, the *quasi-anthropological art* does not fully reassess the issue of art's function for society, it merely replaces the conventional historical types or forms of address with new innovations, new conceptions of the way artworks are made and propositions of what constitutes an artwork (Bruff and Jordan, 2015). In short it advances art in terms of expanding its ontology but does not necessarily address arts political potential. The out-moded figurative representation of *the other* is replaced with an ethical encounter; both leave us with the same questions regarding the ethics of representation and the problems of what Foster calls a 'cultural politics of *marginality*' (Foster, 1995: 303).

At first, when comparing the *social turn* (Bishop, 2012: 11) in art and the *sensory turn* in anthropology (Pink, 2009) the two may appear to converge. The *social turn* in art practice sees artists using methods usually associated with ethnography, including the views and actions of participants as part of the production of final artworks. This aligns with how Sarah Pink describes current ethnographic methods, she says:

> Ethnographic practice tends to include participant observation, ethnographic interviewing, and a range of other participatory research techniques that are often developed and adapted in context and as appropriate to the needs and possibilities afforded by specific research projects. (Pink, 2009: 4)

The *sensory turn* in anthropology, according to Pink enables multiple ways of knowing, rather than employing the classic observational approach which relies on interview. Thus, a sensory ethnographic method would embrace strategies such as visual ethnography, which allows other forms of knowledge to be accessed for research (Pink, 2009: 5). This engagement with the *visual* for ethnographic studies and the employment of ethnographic methods (albeit quasi) to produce artworks associated with the social turn in art, emerge at a similar time.

However, we believe that these parallels are arrived at through isolating art and anthropology's formal characteristics. In this respect *social* art uses methods that are akin to anthropology for the making of artworks; and *sensory* anthropology exploits the processes of technical artistic skill-sharing and (mainly convivial) dialogue in order to engage a participant in a different type of conversation. It seems to us that for those committed to the *sensory turn* in anthropology, the aesthetics of the interpersonal exchange that occurs through the encounter between artist and participant is the key factor of the artwork. This ignores the broader cultural engagement that art brings to social exchange and overlooks the process of transformation through debating, disagreement and difference that occurs through the democratic method of opinion formation in these transactions. The potential of art to function for political and social transformation is what is at stake here. The *sensuous* ethnographer may want to isolate art as a convivial process of exchange in order to affect a *relaxed-type* of conversation, and of course certain artists may agree with this position. However, an emphasis on the convivial aspects of interpersonal exchange limits the potential for a more vigorous exploration of difference, thus producing weaker social relations as a result.

The art historian Claire Bishop goes further, placing the emphasis on arts ability to be antagonistic. Bishop says: 'Without antagonism there is only the imposed consensus of authoritarian order—a total suppression of debate and discussion, which is inimical to democracy.' (Bishop, 2004: 66).

Bishops argues for the consideration of content *and* context in an artwork *as well as* the interpersonal encounter that Nicholas Bourriaud defines as *structure* in his theory of *Relational Aesthetics* (Bourriaud, 2002). In Bishop's terms, 'When confronted by a relational art work, Bourriaud suggests that we ask the following questions: 'does this work permit me to enter into dialogue? Could I exist, and how, in the space it defines?' (Bishop, 2006: 64).

Bishop is disturbed by Bourriaud's remarks because the consequence of his proposed questions mean that the interpersonal relations of an artwork are isolated and the viewer is encouraged to overlook what constitutes the whole artwork; denigrating content and context to a lower position of importance. Bishops says:

> When Bourriaud argues that, 'encounters are more important than the individuals who compose them,' I sense that this question is (for him) unnecessary; all relations that permit *dialogue* are automatically assumed to be democratic and therefore good. But what does *democracy* really mean in this context? If relational art produces human relations, then the next logical question to ask is what types of relations are being produced, for whom, and why?                    (Bishop, 2006: 65).

### 3. Art as politics

Both Foster and Bishop question in which way art can act politically on the social world. Foster is troubled by the way in which a particular type of ethics of representation has been established; one that sets out a pattern which endorses that only those that have lived and experienced oppression can speak to it and of it. This move, in relation to anthropology, takes the customary format of the objective observer and flips it on its head, making the subject and observer one and the same. The consequence of this process is a kind of emptying out of politics from art, not as *content* and *context* as in the case of **Bishop's** critique of Bourriaud, but rather in the form of evacuating action, or to be more specific, limiting the way in which artists can function politically.

When the person that hasn't experienced any suffering or oppression speaks for and towards a particular political cause, why is the first reaction to be dismissive? Is it because we assume that some sort of authenticity of experience is required, that one needs to suffer at the hand of the oppressor in order to protest against the perpetrators acts? This is an example of what Chantal Mouffe describes as 'politics played out in the moral register' (Mouffe, 2005: 75). We simply can not capitulate to an ethic of authentic experience or proximity of cause as a guiding principle to affect protest. Besides, it might be exactly the person that has not experienced the suffering of a set of oppressed others that needs to stand up *with* them. Not only to align themselves with the significance of the cause but to demonstrate their political body being transformed by this new allegiance. Surely this *is* politics.

This challenge is one reason that Foster returns to Benjamin's *Author as producer* (Benjamin, 1970). Benjamin is calling for a productive agency for art; for an art that transforms bourgeois culture by altering the social relations of art itself. He sets out a complex analysis of politics and queries how art and culture operate politically beyond a virtuous approach of ethics and towards an integrated act of politics. He considers who constitutes the collective as well as the actions made by *the individual* for *the collective*. This indicates a move for art, which enables it to progress from ethics to politics; by including the artist as a political body *in action*, whereby *content* and *context*, must be considered. This composition which includes the political act replaces a figurative or pictorial representation of politics. Benjamin describes it as the combination of 'correct political tendency and a progressive literary technique' (Benjamin, 1970: 7). It is Foster's engagement with Benjamin's articulation of the *advanced* artist (Foster, 1995: 302) that suggests at a way through the complexities of representation as he outlines in his essay and it is this approach which informs our proposal for thinking about art and visual ethnography here.

## 4. Social art as visual ethnography

It is useful to examine actual examples of interdisciplinary work to further explore the limitations of the tendency described above. Our purpose here is not to propose correct models of how to make art in this context nor is it to defend one version of art production over another but rather to explore what happens in the various arrangements of when disciplines come together to produce research that engages with participants. Below we briefly review two examples of the way in which art and anthropology, when matched within a research project framework, assume a positive idea of art. We also introduce a project by the Freee art collective entitled *Social Kiosk II* and *Why Map?* that seeks conflicting and therefore political viewpoints from those participants involved.

Artists now commonly work with social scientists encouraged in part by research funding initiatives. It is precisely in this context that we can see the *work* of artists functioning to carry out innovative visual ethnography in which artists provide access to people as subjects most commonly via processes of sharing craft-based technical skills. The Connected Communities programme funded by the Arts and Humanities Research Council is 'a cross-Council programme designed to help us understand the changing nature of communities in their historical and cultural contexts and the role of communities in sustaining and enhancing our quality of life' (AHRC, 2016). Art is seen to have an important role; on the Connected Communities website it states that many of the commissioned research projects aim to include some aspect of 'participatory arts', described as, 'the development of community arts and media and new ways of doing and thinking about practice in participation are focuses for projects that weave together the critical and creative in communities of culture.' (Connected Communities, 2018). Indeed, in their final report Keri Facer and Bryony Enright (Facer and Enright, 2016: 34) provide a brief summary of 'the main approaches, references points and issues that are invoked by both university and community partners in the Connected Communities Programme'. They point out in their literature review what they call a *tradition* of

> Artists and researchers working within the interconnected but distinct fields of participatory arts, community-engaged arts, arts and health, relational aesthetics, critical arts practice and the related but distinct approach within the university of practice as research
>
> (Facer and Enright, 2016: 84).

The Connected Communities projects have various social agendas including; health, work with marginalised groups, therapy, social cohesion and heritage projects. The following accounts of two projects that claim to utilise art and participation in the study; firstly, in the project 'Wonderland: the art of becoming human', 2016, visual anthropologist Dr. Amanda Ravetz, developed an *artistic research project* described as 'by and for people in recovery from substance use disorder and/or mental health issues' that aimed to find out 'how artistic research can further recovery journeys.' (Connected Communities, 2018). In this research project the subject is the photographic portraiture of the practitioner Cristina Nuñez (http://selfportrait-experience.com) and her methods of working with people. The format of this photographic work aims to bring to our attention to specific individuals and their perceived difference through portraiture and self-portraiture, in this case focusing on people experiencing dependence on substance use or with a range of mental health issues.

The artists' workshop, is a common approach to working in healthcare contexts in an economy where practitioners provide creative services as paid work. The project is carried out by the *artist* who applies a type of care and interpersonal interaction which, in this case is focused around the production of a photograph. The sociologist employs ethnography to report on both the method of the artist and through the process the new behaviour of the participant and their resulting behaviour after the project is complete (in some cases the artist is observed). The artist or practitioner so provides a convivial activity for the study wherein people are given space for self-expression via technical skills, a method that could quite easily be replaced with other forms of craft or collective workshop activity, say cooking or drama.

A key issue here in terms of interdisciplinary research work is that of an uneven relationship or asymmetrical dynamic within a research team. This difference is between the practitioner or maker on the one hand and the social scientist on the other. The former is often from outside of academia and their artwork the subject of study, the latter the initiator of the project using the practitioners' work as a means for research. In this relationship questions of arts function or ontology are less likely to be in the foreground as part of the social research project in favour of the effect of the artwork or production process on participants. This is further exacerbated within forms of participatory arts that aim to be 'community-engaged arts' or to deliver on an agenda of arts and health wherein the function for art is unquestionably to provide a positive and beneficial experience for the user. The question for us is, 'Does art practice that aims to be participative enable people to have their collective say; to transform them into critical and empowered subjects that can act together for social justice? Or do the forms of participative art practice used by a research project enact weak or patronising social relations through focusing on the individual narrative and self-representation?' As denoted in the newly conceived term *recoverism*, see www. portraitsofrecovery.org.uk/about/, these questions emanate from arts research and need to be considered when designing interdisciplinary research that alludes to ideas of emancipation for project participants through the engagement with art practice. If these problems are neglected the result is an instrumentalised art that serves sociological research but does not extend ideas of arts function in the development of social justice and collective agency. For an example of a critical community-engaged arts project in which participants were empowered through processes and techniques of art production we can look to the Poster Film Collective, whereby artists worked with marginalised womans' groups to affect equal pay and equal worker's rights for woman see poster-collective.org. uk/women/index.php.

The second example is the project *Taking yourself seriously*, 2015-2018 (Connected Communities, 2018) with principal investigator Kate Pahl, co-investigators Andrew McMillan, Zanib Rasool and collaborators ARVAC; Imagine; TYS. The project sees the development of research from an earlier Connected Communities project *Co-producing legacy*, that sought to produce resources that established arts methodologies when used in the voluntary and community sector. Here artists are framed as having methodologies that were 'founded on tacit, experiential, visual and linguistic knowledge that are open to change and can be experimental' (Connected Communities, 2018). The artistic methodologies are described as useful in developing ideas of cohesion when working in practical community projects, in this case, designing an adventure playground, working with a school and with a group of Muslim women (Figure 5.1). The original project *Co-producing legacy* included Helen Graham academic expert on museum studies and access for people with learning difficulties and freelance artist Steve Pool.

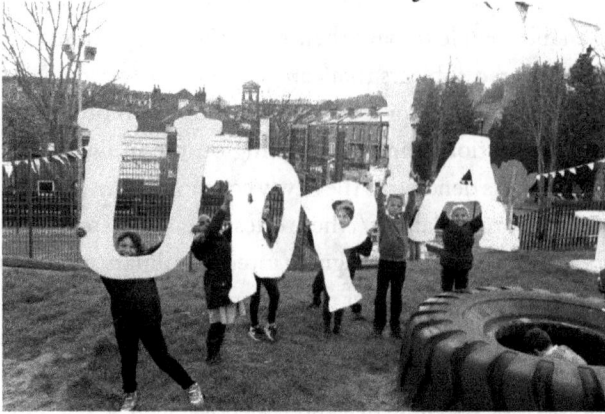

Figure 5.1: The Utopia Project, 2017. Pitsmoor Adventure Playground.[1]

In this project practices of relational working common to social art practice become part of the process of finding solutions to urban community issues. In the UK since the 1990s social cohesion projects in poorer neighbourhoods have regularly used artists as catalysts for change as part of urban development, often called culture-led regeneration. The activity of art professionals then become communication tools in support of community development. The issue in this process is that without engaging with all the political aspects affecting the community concerned the art project acts as a means to support a top down agenda usually set by the governing agencies leading the regeneration plan with the artist commissioned to enact a brief (Hewitt, 2011: 24). The history of critical and political social practice gives us instances of artwork that are reflexive to the contexts in which they operate and in conjunction with those people working and living in these contexts. An instance would be the *Docklands Community Poster Project* by artists Peter Dunn and Lorraine Leeson in which residents developed content for campaigns on social and environmental issues affecting them, some of which became photomurals (www.arte-ofchange.com/content/docklands-community-poster-project-1981-8) (Figure 5.2). Social art practice then operates as a space for open democratic exchange whereby people can form their own position. In contra-distinction, interdisciplinary research projects working in a community aim for positive solutions with art instrumentalised to meet that end. In this example, partners also include charity

1. Connected Communities 2018 with principal investigator Kate Pahl, co-investigators Andrew McMillan, Zanib Rasool and collaborators ARVAC; Imagine; TYS. Source: https://connected-communities.org/index.php/project/taking-yourselves-seriously/

and third sector agencies, civil society groups that are also regular patrons for participatory art to help aid their policy interests.

Figure 5.2: Peter Dunn and Loraine Leeson, Docklands Community Poster Project, 1982-85. Image three from the first series of eight 18' x 12' (5.49m x 3.66m) photo-murals—The Changing Picture of Docklands.

So, despite the well-established discourse on arts and regeneration this does not feature in interdisciplinary research. Is this a consequence of artistic projects being led by social scientists? In this situation the researcher-lead becomes the commissioner or patron of the artistic work thereby setting the parameters of the art production despite not being an art specialist, either academic, curator or practitioner. Does the social scientist then subsume or even recuperate the critical agency of the social art practice to meet their own priorities?

Art and its participative trends were framed by Nicolas Bourriaud in his influential book *Relational aesthetics* (Bourriaud, 2002) and now nearly twenty years later, social practice is routinely used in various institutional settings, including by interdisciplinary research teams. Such projects can then mimic forms and conventions of art practice whilst paying scant attention to key aspects of the disciplinary discourse. Certainly, the work done in such projects is not testing or extending new ideas of art.

The projects in the Connected Communities initiative affirmed the usefulness of art across 'a number of disciplinary fields including art therapy, social work, community health, cultural policy and geographies of health.' (AHRC, 2016) As in the first example, arts related activity, including craft skills, making and discursive pedagogic techniques are commonly used to tackle the needs of specific social groups or communities of interest through workshop processes. The focus of the work is that of wellbeing, of giving space for people to engage with professionals to overcome personal issues. Therefore, the use of arts related activity including ideas of participation in this context has a specific function to alleviate identified problems and is a form of social and personal amelioration. The function of art-based activity is to provide a benefit to those with particular needs like many of the projects funded by Connected Communities. Questions of arts social potential as a space for critical engagement on political, social or philosophical issues is neglected despite those matters being central to the discourse on the art and the social turn (Bishop, 2006).

What these examples demonstrate is just how common the aim for a positive and functional role for art in research projects is, when art and anthropology come together. What is then surprising is the reference to critical forms of art in the literature associated with the research project Connected Communities. Included in Facer and Enright's report are reference to key theorists of arts *social turn*, that of Claire Bishop (Bishop, 2006), Nicholas Bourriaud (Bourriaud, 2002) and Grant Kester (Kester, 2011). The authors flag up the discourse on participative art, the very discourse that has problematised the instrumentalisation of art and social relations of art, despite, and this is our assertion, that their work for Connected Communities reproduces this problem.

Bishop (2012) has described the *social turn* in art, the expanded field of relational practices, primarily in the globalised arena of art biennials supported by the public sector. Bishop describes how proponents of socially-engaged art practice have attempted to shift art from its traditional exclusive constituency to make it more inclusive and *socially relevant*. One way in which artists have challenged art's function is to work in non-art contexts (outside of the gallery) and with non-art audiences. Although this move by artists is motivated by the desire to transform the nature of art practice and can be seen as ontological, as we described above, each shift into a new form of practice brings with a new set of considerations so this new engagement with non-art publics has made art seemingly more useful and more likely to be instrumentalised by the Government in seeking solutions to urban socio-economic problems and in this case, through the work of social scientists funded by research councils.

On closer examination of the instances of participatory art projects cited in the Connected Communities literature, reflection on the social turn in art to include antagonistic encounters is lacking, the critical and historical issues of cultural production apparent in such discourse become muted in favour of positivist conceptions of art enabling the *weaving* of communities together through activity-led participation. One instance where the social turn is used is in the Connected Communities sponsored book entitled, *Valuing interdisciplinary collaborative research: Beyond impact*, edited by Keri Facer and Kate Pahl (Facer and Pahl, 2017). Their aim is to examine how Universities (arts, humanities and social sciences) are increasingly active in collaborating with citizens and community organisations. In the chapter entitled 'What is the role of artists in interdisciplinary collaborative projects with universities and communities?' (Pahl et al., 2017) they provide a literature review on the history of social art practice including the influential Artists Placement Group, arts social turn (Bishop, 2012) and socially engaged artists working under New Labour in projects such as Creative Partnerships. Interestingly, the researchers state that they are aware of how artists can be disenfranchised via academic and community projects, describing how the artists' epistemologies can remain 'hidden within projects'. It is notable then, that the projects they initiate reproduce this very problem.

Pahl et al., (2017) provide three case studies, which highlight artists' views when taken from conversations with the researchers. In the project 'Workshops: Ways of knowing', they describe the processes and communications between artists and researchers in art-based workshops (Pool, Holland, Hill) as a 'disorientation' between academics and professionals. Discussions were said to have broken down, becoming 'more edgy' leading to the 'discussion on the role that artists can play in unsettling and disrupting' (ibid.144). The authors then theorise this edginess as a form of *dissensus* quoting Chantelle Mouffe's theory of agonism (Mouffe, 2005). Despite this framing of artistic practices in rather radical and politicised terms in the literature review, we want to understand why this is so absent in the case studies mentioned in their report and also within the majority of Connected Community projects? Pahl and her co-authors place any such disorientation from artistic activity as more likely 'felt' and not said which is a move from the linguistic and social toward the sensual and individual, a move which could be said to be at odds with the concept of art and the *social turn*.

There is evidence here of an imbalance between the interests of art research and that of social scientists in these interdisciplinary projects. Within interdisciplinary projects social scientists are framing the production of art and its function within social contexts in teams that lack knowledge and experience on the nuances of art production, its histories and theories. This absence can then lead to the utilisation of art simply as a means for social science research to reproduce a conception of art that assumes a universally beneficial function for social good and fails to acknowledge the critical and contested characteristics of art practice. Reviewing all the Connected Communities project we could not find one academic whose research was based in social art practice, an art historian or a curating academic among the PrincipalInvestigator or Co-Investigators.

By way of contrast and as an instance of an alternative approach we will briefly discuss a work by the Freee art collective, of which the authors are both members and one that goes some way to recognise and bridge differences in the interdisciplinary approaches to research. As part of the project the *Freee-Carracci-Institute* at NN Contemporary in Northampton in November 2016 we made the artwork *Free Kiosk #2* (Beech, Hewitt and Jordan, 2016). During the project we developed an interdisciplinary research project between Freee and the Centre for Democratic Practices (CfDP, a research group at the University of Northampton, academics from Business and Law, Psychology, Cultural Studies and International business students). The research sought to investigate how the public of Northampton had reached their voting decisions in the recent referendum to leave the EU. The data gathering, the first stage of the project collected the public's reasoning about their arguments. The emphasis here was on the opinion formation process, rather than making a value judgment about the decisions people had made. The artwork consisted a mobile kiosk structure designed by Freee from which the researchers gathered data from passersby in the Market Square in Northampton (Figure 5.3). From the data a graphic designer produced the *Why? Map* to visually communicate the respondent's views. The *Why? Map* is a discursive tool and is added to by others respondents whenever it is displayed in the public realm (Figure 5.4).

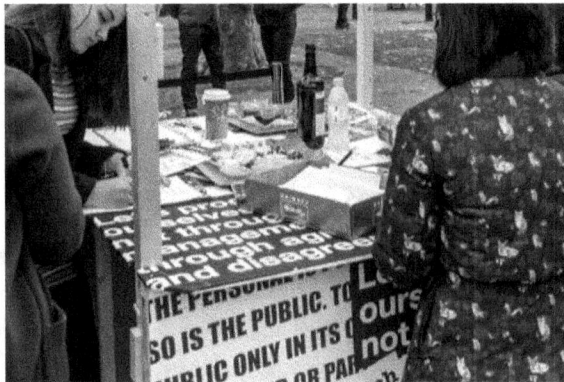

Figure 5.3: Freee and the Centre for Democratic Practices (CfDP) The University of Northampton. Freee Kiosk #2 (open) with the *Why? Map*, installation in Market Square, Northampton, 2016. Photograph by Joe Brown.

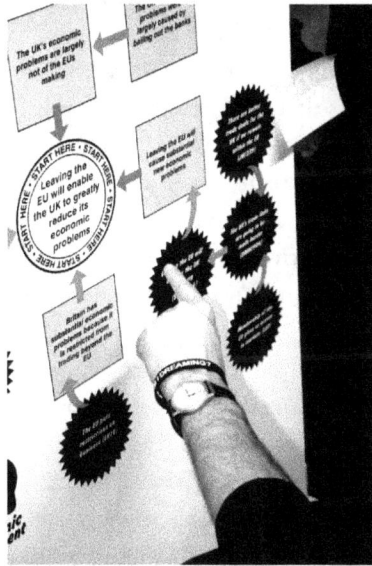

Figure 5.4: Freee and the Centre for Democratic Practices (CfDP) The University of Northampton. Photograph by Freee. *Why? Map* by Graham Smith, design by Alexis Taylor, on the 'Freee Slogan Stand', 2016.

This collaborative work was a partnership based on agreed objectives and content, with opinion formation as a common topic between all the researchers involved. It is an instance of artists as key agents in an antagonistic project that they design and perform. Similarly, the testing of the critical conceptions of what art is and does runs through the research, the art is not static or a given model, a technical exercise in making art that will provide an audience to study. Such art research is then following a trajectory of the avant-garde and the social turn in which art is reflexive to the social conditions in which it is produced. This is cultural production as essentially a dialogical process between people as a politicised exchange of opinions, values and meaning. This project went some way to test a collective process of working amongst researchers with a number of shared political and ideological positions.

## 5. Conclusion

The two examples of projects we discuss from the AHRC Connected Communities programme provide instances of some of these problematics; namely the designation of artist being hired as specialists or practitioners but not as critical research partners. There were no artist researchers, art historians or curators supported to lead these projects, which is surprising since the rise in practice-led PhDs has increased since the 1990s. We can see that artists can be put to work on projects that seek outcomes or solutions for social cohesion or amelioration despite the problems we raise in this approach—the emphasis given to individual recovery rather than longer term solutions and without reference to discourses on art and politics. In the final project we report on a project by the Freee art collective that attempts to work within a social context and address the politics of art and culture through interdisciplinary interventions in the public domain.

Given the increase in social and participatory artworks produced in context of what Claire Bishop has named as the *social turn*—derived from her 2006 essay *The social turn: Collaboration and Its discontents* (Bishop, 2012:11)—it was timely to return to Hal Foster's 1995 essay *Artist as ethnographer?* (Foster, 1995), and explore some of his original concerns of art and its engagement with the social. Foster reminds us of Benjamin's writing on the social production of art, in particular his concept of technique which he describes as 'correct political tendency and a progressive literary technique' (Benjamin, 1970: 7). For Benjamin, *tendency* is the general direction a writer or her work takes, whether political or literary and *technique* represents the technical means by which a work is produced, its means of production, here aligned very closely to technology.

Benjamin's efforts in both his essays, *Author as producer* (Benjamin, 1970) and *The work of art in the age of mechanical reproduction* (Benjamin, 1969) describes the practice of art as having the agency to change the way we act, what we do and how we behave (Jordan, 2017). In his essay *Aesthetic ground of critical theory* (Bertram, 2015), Georg W Bertram claims that 'Benjamin introduces the concept of *aura* in a context in which he comes to speak about questions of perceptions' (Bertram, 2015: 2), this enables Benjamin 'to conceive that sensuous perception is historically determined' (Bertram, 2015: 2). This does two things: first, it moves the artwork away from an essentialist positioning: e.g. applying this approach no artworks can be essentially beautiful; and second, it situates the artwork in a social continuum, which calls our attention to the idea of behaviour and perception as a socially determined practice. (Jordan, 2017)

Foster is no doubt perturbed with the arrangement of art and anthropology and the crisis of representation, or what he calls, a 'cultural politics of *marginality*' (Foster, 1995: 303). We argue that this predicament is an ethical evaluation of the function of art practice as opposed to a critical or political arrangement. This has resonance with the critique of objectivity as supposedly brought by the social science researcher to community contexts. It is this discussion between ethics and politics that aligns with some of the criticism that Bishop makes of Bourriaud's (2002) *Relational aesthetics* and we utilise this to explore the rise in artworks made within research projects that are dominated by social science researchers.

We have outlined how interdisciplinary research can *use* art and the work of artists, as a means to study communities in the work of social science. This can occur through research funding mechanisms that favour a social science agenda; as a consequence of this the complex questions central to art and its social function remain unconsidered and left undiscussed. In general, social scientists are not trained in the study of arts' practice and the contingencies of production and more crucially its application. As we discuss in the examples above the social scientist researcher generates a project that speaks of the theories of the social turn but fails to understand how this might manifest in the production of artworks. Thus the social science researcher invites artists to carry out artworks that employ *techniques* of participatory production, rather than those artists that produce artworks in tandem with the emerging discourse around the social turn. This is an example of the risks inherent in interdisciplinary research and demonstrates how misrecognitions can occur.

In conclusion we would like to propose the following for the interdisciplinary practice of art and sociology:

> An acknowledgement of the difference between socially engaged art projects that support individual recovery and those that aim to achieve collective social change.

> The promotion of collective working as opposed to collaboration; that shared values of disciplines, organisations / art institutions, etc. are established so that the artworks are not employed as a means of visual ethnography but operate towards a number of political and ideological values.

> New interdisciplinary methodologies for evaluation of social art projects; that include engagement with and reference to art theories, histories and practices, politics and pedagogy. Real-time ethnographies that consider contingent conditions of a project and its participants. It is this entanglement of conditions and reflexive responses that need to be discussed through reflective means such as ethnography.

# References

AHRC., (2016) 'Connected communities', Accessed: August 13th 2018. http://www.ahrc.ac.uk/research/fundedthemesandprogrammes/crosscouncilprogrammes/connectedcommunities/

Beech, D., Hewitt, A. and Jordan, M. (eds.), (2017) *The Carracci Institute Year Book*, Northampton: NN Contemporary.

Benjamin, W., (1970 [1934]) Author as producer (translated by John Heckman), *New Left Review*, 1(62):1-9.

Benjamin, W., (1969 [1936]) The work of art in the age of mechanical reproduction, in Arendt, H., (ed.) *Illuminations*, New York: Schocken.

Bertram, G., (2015) Benjamin and Adorno on art as critical practice, in Ross, N., (ed.) *Aesthetic ground of critical theory: New readings of Benjamin and Adorno*, London: Rowman and Littlefield.

Bishop, C., (2004) Antagonism and relational aesthetics, *October*, 110:51-79.

Bishop, C., (2012) *Artificial hells: Participatory art and the politics of spectatorship*, London: Verso.

Bourriaud, N,. (2002) *Relational aesthetics*, Dijon: Les Presses du Réel

Connected Communties., (2018) 'Participatory art', Accessed: 13 August, 13th, 2018. https://connected-communities.org/index.php/cluster/participatory-arts-2/

Facer, K. and Pahl, K. (eds.), (2017) *Valuing interdisciplinary collaborative research: Beyond impact*. Bristol: Policy Press.

Facer, K. and Enright, B. (2016) *Creating living knowledge: The connected communities programme, community-university partnerships and the participatory turn in the production of knowledge*, Bristol: Arts and Humanities Research Council.

Foster, H., (1995) The artist as ethnographer?, in Marcus, G. and Myers, F., (eds.) *Refiguring art and anthropology*, Berkeley: University of California Press.

Hewitt, A., (2011) Privatizing the public: Three rhetorics of art's public good in 'Third Way' cultural policy, *Art and the Public Sphere*, 1(1):19-36.

Jordan, M., (2017) Towards critical practices: Art and design as socially productive practices, in Linda King, L. and Oonagh Young, O., (eds.) *Transdisciplinary practice*, Dublin: O. Young Gallery.

Jordan, M. and Bruff, I., (2015) Rethinking the artistic imagination, *The 12th European Sociological Association Conference (ESA)*, 25-28 August, Prague.

Kester, G., (2011) *The one and the many: Contemporary collaborative art in a global context*, California: Duke University Press.

Mouffe, C., (2005) *On the political*, London: Routledge.

Pahl, K., Escott, H., Graham, H., Marwood, K., Pool, S. and Ravetz, A., (2017) What is the role of artists in interdisciplinary collaborative projects with universities and communities?, in Facer, K. and Pahl, K., (eds.) *Valuing interdisciplinary collaborative research: Beyond impact*, Bristol: Policy Press.

Pink, S., (2009) *Doing sensory ethnography*, London: Sage.

Rockhill, G., (2014) *Radical history and the politics of art*, New York: Columbia University Press.

# Chapter 6

# Ethnotheatre: Expanding participant observation

*Ricardo Seiça Salgado*

## 1. Introduction: Locating ethnotheatre

Ethnotheatre is an art-based methodology connecting ethnography and theatre. It is a method to dramatise personal, cultural and social observations and arguments of real life in a given context. Working with and about the life of others, ethnotheatre may stand simultaneously as methodology and object of ethnographic practice. It combines collection of data, interpretation and analysis with research action through theatre. On the other hand, it has the potential to empower the participants of research, enabling social action as a definitional ceremony (Myerhoff, 1982). I am going to discuss how ethnotheatre may expand participant observation and contribute to the amplification of the ethnographic method. I will use some ethnographic evidence from an ongoing ethnotheatre research project in a prison and an ethnotheatre project I have done with members of an old university theatre group, called CITAC (Coimbra's Academy Theatrical Initiation Circle) (Salgado, 2007, 2013, 2014).

In the late eighties of the twentieth century there was a movement in anthropology that understood culture as performance, more as a verb than as a name, and which characterised the performative turn of ethnographic thinking—also coined as a reflexive turn (Alexander, 2005; Conquergood, 1998; Ruby, 1982; Turner and Turner, 1982). Fieldwork progressively became a collaborative process (Lassiter, 2005; Estalella and Criado, 2015; Finley, 2005), a more performative than informative knowledge. As Glenn Hinson (in Lassiter, 2005: 17) highlights, collaboration is more radical than reciprocation. In the ethnographic process, reciprocation 'sets up a model of exchange where one thing granted (e.g., an interview) yields an appropriate reciprocal response (e.g., help planting a garden)' (ibid.). Collaboration implies constant 'mutual engagement at every step of the process' (ibid.) and this is what sets collaboration apart from reciprocation.

This change towards a more collaborative attitude, as we shall see, it is a consequence of devised theatre or collaborative work. But this shift also occurred in the avant-garde theatre movement, in the long sixties (a period that extends the sixties up to the eighties of the twentieth century) (Schechner, 2015). The art of performance grasps several changes:

1) The authority of the dramatic text ends. There is now a space for contemporary social issues to govern the staging process.

2) The performer frees himself from the character that the text would define and embarks on the creation of a persona. "In acting, or playing a character, you want to impersonate the personality of a person that is not yourself. A persona, however, is an artifact, a fabrication, that corresponds to what you want to project from yourself, from within. It is like taking a facet, a fragment, and using that as a seed to elaborate on. It is you and yet not you—a part of you but not the whole. It is not a lie but neither the full truth." (Rosenthal, quoted in Lampe, 2002: 296-297). We could also define the anthropologist in the fieldwork as a persona (Salgado, 2016). In a way, the traditional exercise of academic writing always implied it, but it is now more relevant that the construction of the persona implies a kind of auto-ethnography. This presence as a persona becomes a game and an interplay between different research roles in the field and modes of documentation, always in negotiation while doing collaborative ethnography. Partly, it is a direct consequence of practicing participant observation. When one does an observation, the tendency is to decrease the level of participation. The possibilities and efficacy of eliciting data is enriched by this awareness or focus on the kind of presence that a specific role plays in the frame of any encounter.

3) The performance is a more democratic and participative event, as in the collective creations of devised theatre. When applied to the research, there is a dilution of the researcher role as *credentialed expert*—according to Snow et al. (2001) in their categorisation of researchers' roles. When activating the public as performer, there is a tendency to break the fourth wall and to perform real social dramas by confronting the public, ultimately, with direct action. This kind of work implies a previous research on the addressed themes and problems, nourished by the spirit of collaboration.

In the academy, the performative turn goes along with the emergence of performance studies. Victor and Edie Turner (1982) propose a pedagogical stance to their students, the dramatisation of ethnographic description of rituals. This vision implied the development of theatrical scripts along with ethnographic texts, and then perform for educational purposes. Eugenio Barba develops ISTA (International School of Theatre Anthropology) to research the universal foundations of performance and work with the masters of the various theatrical traditions around the world. Others, like Della Pollock, Howard Becker, Michal McCall (Denzin, 1997), or Dwight Conquergood (1985), instead of reading the scientific papers, began to perform scripts from their ethnographies. They could play themselves or also use parts of their interlocutors, or even dramatise observed rituals. This was the terrain for the emergence of ethnotheatre.

## 2. Defining ethnotheatre

In the twenty-first century, we enter the performance of ethnography with the formalisation of ethnotheatre as both method and expression of a research project. The performance of the ethnography encounters other operative modes of doing participant observation. Briefly, ethnotheatre is a subgenre of documentary theatre. It connects ethnographic methods (it is an alternative mode of participant observation) and theatrical or choreographic methodologies. In a given context of analysis, it is a way of dramatising observations and arguments about personal, social and cultural life. It can be both a methodology and/or an object of the practice of ethnography: it is a methodology when the process of construction of the play is itself the methodology of the research, focusing on specific vernacular fields of knowledge; it is an object of ethnography, when we make an ethnography to the theatrical process as such. In any case, the ethnographic research is, therefore, preparatory fieldwork for a theatrical production.

Ethnotheatre promotes opportunities for anthropologists, artists and the public to open and sustain communication in the darkest, most complex and confusing areas of sociocultural reality. It allows an examination of the experiences of others in the democratic forum that is theatre. It stimulates reflexivity, fostering a broader discussion of the politics of representation and identity that crosses all systems of oppression. On the other hand, ethnotheatre must consider who is speaking in the name of whom, actively linking the politics of culture that regulate which characteristics and elements of culture must be presented or suppressed.

The methodology of ethnotheatre bases itself on the joint process of obtaining, sharing and projecting knowledge, with an important pedagogical and communicative potential. The challenge is to project knowledge of the other without controlling the experience of the other. It is also an aim of this kind of ethnotheatre to break the fourth wall of the theatre, seeking to create, in the wake of Bertolt Brecht (n. d.) or Augusto Boal (2005), a more dialectical theatre. And here, we may contribute to a democratisation of knowledge, working also with a wider public, not confined to the academy. It is widely known that different theatre methodologies have different laboratory procedures. They activate different cognitive mechanisms as well as affective potential. Each theatrical methodology triggers different modes of relating with oneself and the world. Therefore, on one hand, ethnotheatre leads the way to the context we want to work with and on the other hand different theatre methodologies may allow distinct collection, type or quality of ethnographic data.

Using certain methods of composition may not be suitable for social science research, such as in some forms of dance that rely on already existing formal or rigid motion vocabularies, so they don't allow the research of the local or vernacular vocabularies (Blumenfeld-Jones, 2008). We may use a distinct methodology as, for instances, the theatre of the oppressed developed by Augusto Boal (2005) to elicit situations of oppression everybody lived or were involved with at some point of their lives. The researcher becomes the facilitator, the joker. He collects real events and gathers everybody's interpretations on that matter. The rehearsal is the context to debate and express each view about such immediate political situation.

We can work on the research themes in more subtle ways like when using viewpoints or clown technique, for instances. When using the viewpoints methodology (Bogart and Landau, 2005) with a group of young inmates, I found great potential to set an improvisational system in a play about the lifecycle of being in a prison, which is my current project. Focusing on the viewpoint *space* is very different of focusing on viewpoint *time* during any improvisation. Different aspects of reality emerge. Therefore, we can strategically use different theatre methodologies for different approaches to the topic we are researching. The good thing is that the quality of ethnographic data tends to be surprising. The participants have to collectively define themselves through this definitional ceremony (Myerhoff, 1982), a ceremony that would otherwise not exist. When the participants are involved in the creative process there is enough space for processes of emergence, while putting culture in motion (Rosaldo, 1993; Conquergood, 1998). This is also a new form of thinking about the process of inquiring.

The common goal of ethnotheatre is to research a particular aspect of the community with the purpose of adapting these observations and knowledge to the construction of an aesthetic performance. It implies the construction of an ethnodrama, hopefully a script built by all the participants of the research project. In order to make a distinction from conventional, fictional dramatic literature,

Saldaña (2011) lists four distinct approaches to ethnodramatic playwriting. I take them as a structure to organise and develop my view on ethnodrama as an ethnographic device:

1)     Ethnodramatic adaptations of documents and published accounts. This approach to build an ethnodrama may use autobiographical, biographical, and historical textual materials, fieldnotes, media documents, journals, blogs, correspondence, cds, everything that supposedly resists change, whether primary or secondary sources. It is what Diana Taylor (2007) calls the archive. As she says, the archive is, in a way, immune to change. What changes over time is the value, the relevance, the meaning of the document (and its ability to produce partial connections to the overall theme of analysis pursued by any researcher). What changes over time is how the researcher interprets or even embodies the elements that compose any document.

As Taylor argues, the archive operates in the same way as any written theatrical text. There are multiple ways of representing any dramatic text. You have to create a specific dramaturgy and staging. A different staging may result in a completely different spectacle or experience, although the dramatic text remains unchanged. If we are working in an adaptation of different archive material and the participants of that research are the performers of the play, we gain an expertise on the interpretation of documents, because we can combine the information coming from the *repertoire* (Taylor, 2007), or the testimonies of someone who lived the same event that the document refers to. Of course, when we are using problematical information to the subjects, it may be better to avoid mentioning the archive.

We may find the roots of ethnodramatic adaptations of documents in Piscator's *Epic Theatre* (just before Brecht developed the concept) (Innes, 1972; Piscator, 1995; Vasques, 2007). Here, ethnodrama emerges from authentic documents and sources of known historical situations (newspapers, articles, reports, and all kind of informational documents). In this kind of theatre, there is also the introduction of several performative devices such as the figure of the narrator-commentator; the projection of documentary films in-between or inside the scenes; the inclusion of photographs that aims to express the portrayed social reality; or even simple document-texts or drawings. These projections also have the function of commenting, inaugurating a kind of *physical materiality* to the commentary. It was also possible to build complex scenography devices serving the persuasive purposes of the dramatic structure (and not merely scenography for decoration), as the moving scenario or several scenes being performed simultaneously (for Piscator innovations in theatre see Innes, 1972; Vasques, 2007).

2)      Original autoethnodramatic work is when autobiography becomes autoethnodrama. Several dramaturges as Spalding Gray, or researchers as Tamy Spry developed one-person-shows that we may call autoethnodramas.

> Autoethnographic performance is the convergence of the *autobiographic impulse* and the *ethnographic moment* represented through movement and critical self-reflexive discourse in performance, articulating the intersections of peoples and culture through the inner sanctions of the always migratory identity                    (Spry, 2001: 706).

This research writing and method connects the personal experience and memory with culture and social contexts, the starting point for writing. It has performative emancipatory potential as a method of inquiry. Unlike the experience of fictional theatre, there is no *suspending disbelief*. In autoethnodrama, we are 'assuming belief' (Saldaña, 2011: 24).

Recently, the notion of performativity states that an identity (or any autobiographical story) is not just something a person elects to do but it produces an effect on the subject it appears to express (Butler, 1993). Likewise, an autobiographical story is created and recreated in the very moment it is being told. It is impossible to separate it from the social, cultural or political contexts in which it is created, recreated or presented (different publics may have different interpretations). This also attests why ethnotheatre may be the object of ethnography (from the emotional to the political). Performativity relies on performance to express itself (Langellier, 1999).

The method of autoethnography also becomes part of the tradition that defines *anthropology at home*. Autoethnography has a double sense: a) it refers to an ethnography of one's own culture. The *home* culture that constitutes the *insider* view in autoanthropology does not necessarily match the knowledge or interpretation of other *natives*. As Strathern (1987) advices, there are particular techniques of writing ethnographic texts that compose its genre of knowing, its specific organisation of knowledge, or its management of data in specific ways. This use of ethnography as method is one of the most important features to differentiate anthropology from other disciplines, because it configures its epistemology. Quoting Asad, Strathern (1987: 28) says that *models, structures, systems* are apprehended not simply as objectifications, but as result of how data is organised; b) Autoethnography also refers to autobiographical writing with an ethnographic interest (Reed-Danahay, 1997). In this view, a common subject expressed by autoethnographers is the phenomenon of cultural displacement, for instances a situation of exile or emigration. Even if they are not really at home, they compose home.

From my perspective, autoethnodramatic writing invites the notion of performative writing (Phelan, 1998; Pollock, 1998). Instead of being the description of a performative event as *direct representation*, performative writing takes over the affective and the political force of that performative event. According to Pollock, this writing is reflexive, and questions the stability of the ideologically constituted meanings. And it is metonymic. In its own materiality, performative writing underlines the phenomenon based on the corporeal, the affective. It simultaneously addresses scenes and expresses what motivated it, recreating, marking and transforming. Thus, it is not neutral. It does not describe an objectively verified event or process as in the traditional sense. It uses language as an act of painting to create what is more or less self-evident, a version of what has been, or what is, elaborating it in the presence of the writer (or his/her persona). But it also moves and operates through scientific writing, it implies the deconstruction of discursive formations. It evokes worlds that otherwise were intangible or voiceless. And it does so in a partial, multivocal way, being also consequent, in the sense of being an aesthetic, ethical and a political attitude.

3)　　　The third approach to ethnodramatic playwriting Saldaña (2011) refers to is the dramatisation of interview transcripts. With this method, interlocutors may perform its own interview but also other performers can do it. Taylor (2007) calls the *repertoire* to the knowledge coming from the experience of the interlocutors that lived the events we are studying. There are many advantages in connecting and relating the knowledge coming from the *archive* with the *repertoire*. In an ethnotheatre project I made as part of an ethnography to the university theatre group called CITAC, I conducted formal interviews with the older members of the different generations from 1956, when the group was born (Salgado, 2013; 2014). The current generation of CITAC were the actors for this play, revisiting their own history. The recorded interviews of the older members became part of a documentary film I made about the group (Salgado, 2007). For the new members, these interviews were also the juice or ethnographic data to create the dramaturgy of the theatre play, helping also to compose the characters or personae of each scene.

In the film, our purpose was to find an ethos that would characterise the group members since its emergence and how they become protagonists of the student's movement of the sixties. This ethos echoes avant-garde theatre and political resistance to dictatorship, and a sense of transgression, of rebellion, of inconformity, in art and in life. In the beginning of the theatre play we staged, the current actors re-enact on stage the interview we also used for the documentary. The ex-members of the group inspired the characters played by the actual actors. They build a dramaturgy to interpret the interview made of the older members. In a way we made a kind of multimodal (inter)action analysis[1] (Norris, 2016) while watching the recorded interviews of these ex-members that would inspire our dramatic scene.

Multimodal (inter)action analysis investigates interaction. To use its grammar, while watching the interviews, we paid attention to the several lower-level mediated action, as methodological tools such as postures, gestures, gaze, intonation and pitch. We needed to understand a common cultural system of mediated action. As such, we had to combine 'multiple socio-cultural, cognitive and psychological, embodied, physical, and semiotic mediational means/cultural tools' (Norris, 2016: 160). This would characterise the different generations of this theatre group. All the interviewers had common higher-level mediated actions (engaging in research project; relating with the camera; interacting with the interviewer or, sometimes an audience of interviewers; relating to the environment, usually their home or workplace; or answering the same questions we prepared for the interview). This allowed us to study the communicative context of the interviews and the metacommunicative features as the stylistic cues embedded in their messages (gaze, gestures, reactions to a question or a comment, proxemics, etc.). Our aim, then, was to express these lower-level mediated actions in the performance, echoing the same mediational cultural tools.

The interviewers lived in a time of censorship. One of our aims was to decipher hidden transcripts (Scott, 1990), information that is characterised by the interlocutors to make any social critique in the backstage of public life. We were translating some of the parallel epistemologies people had developed as a mode of resistance. To find the group's ethos, we studied the attitude of distinct

1. I thank David Poveda for questioning how I studied the metacommunicative context of these interviews, confronting me with a multimodal (inter)action analysis. Naturally, I am responsible for any consideration about the methodology.

members of different generations of CITAC, during the several social dramas or student crises against dictatorship. Then we combined with the personal attitude we learned viewing the interviews and gathering several lower-level mediated actions, later used to build the characters. This also taught us a lot about the ethos or cultural personality of belonging of this theatre group.

In the creative process, it occurred to me to get the actors to *represent* themselves in the last scene of the play, as if they were mimicking the situation of being interviewed by an anthropologist, equivalent to what we have done in the first scene to the older members. I invited them to build a persona of themselves. They wrote the script of their answers to a hypothetical question the public could not hear. They composed the information they felt was more relevant and meaningful to account for their position in the group, the art world, the academy, and the world in which they lived. This technique gave insightful accounts for the ethos they also were discovering and building within the group. This is an example of dialogic and collaborative work in ethnotheatre as research-action. It also provided a collective self-definition to an audience not otherwise available (Meyerhoff, 1982).

The answers of this fictional interview were given to me without even asking the questions. Of course, they inspired themselves in the interviews to the older members, using the same interview's structure. But they had the freedom to improvise during five minutes each, about the meaningful stories and their experiences in the group, or the positions in the academy and what they learned with and within the group. In the rehearsals, this allowed me to analyse the mediational cultural tools, and discuss with them the answers they were giving to me during the improvisation process. These focus-group sessions gave the opportunity to record multiple fieldnotes that I used for ethnographic analysis (texts, photographs, videos).

4)     Finally, Saldaña (2011) talks about the devised theatre or collaborative work, a collective creation of an ethnodrama as an approach to ethnodramatic playwriting. I have an open view of devised theatre. We can inspire ourselves in a social drama, a social problem or a conflict, a fictional book or a movie, or just improvise about any theme we agree to work with, as a tactic to explore sociocultural dimensions of the participants. As I practice it, the actors are also the interlocutors of the ethnographic project. The researcher takes the role of facilitator or director, and everybody engages a collaborative work. He may use any improvisation technique to elicit data and material for the construction

of the theatre play. The participants are both interviewee, performers of daily life and performers performing themselves. They may also contribute to the gathering of information or ethnographic data, both as an autoethnography or *doing participant observation* as well. We gather the re-collected data at the rehearsals. As we will see, this kind of theatre process has great implications on the knowledge of how to do participant observation, as well as on the features and repercussions of the research.

### 3. Expanding participant observation

Methodologically speaking, practicing ethnotheatre with devised theatre as I defined it above expands the possibilities of the fieldwork techniques. When traditional methodologies are intrinsically limited to the nature of the research context, as it happens in a prison, you are limited to formal interviews or, more rarely, having unrestricted access to prisoners (Cunha, 2014; Frois, 2017). Ultimately, ethnographic theatre practices allow access to the terrain in a way that would otherwise be impossible. Opportunities for such type of encounters with the participants in the study could not happen without these artistic practices. Entering the ethnographic context is variable but can become very challenging. In a prison ethnography, the researcher role would be easily limited to the *observer-as-a-participant* (Gold, 2001), attached to the role of the *credentialed expert* (Snow et al., 2001). In this case, the record would be restricted to transcription, audio, or video recording of the interview.

The performativity of the methodology activates a pertinent sensitivity for the quality of ethnography. We have to hold the play and management of the anthropologist's roles in the field as an essential component of fieldwork. In order to do fieldwork in a prison, my access was formally prepared as a credentialed expert that was going to make a theatre project. The credentialed expert role corresponds to the persona based on the identity of the professional anthropologist. There is no dissimulation, but the obvious manifestation of the professional status. This role is effective in legitimising the presence in the field and even in legitimising other roles that we might want to use to increase participation, as the theatre director's one. I use mostly the credentialed expert role when interacting with the institutional interlocutors (social and psychological workers belonging to the *staff* may also frame me in between the theatre director's role). The inmates mostly see me as the theatre teacher. The relationship I want to produce with the *staff* members of the institution is not the same as with the inmates or even the prison guards, a different group in the prison population. We are not obliged to use the same role with different elements of the research context (not even with the same interlocutor, in different phases of the research).

Different roles of the researcher allow different types of encounter that, in turn, activate the data differently. While combining theatrical methodologies with ethnography, the researcher assumes the role of a director, a member of a team that collectively builds a spectacle or a film, blurring the status of the credentialed expert role. For the inmates, the research purposes are also clear but the frame of the theatre director speaks louder than the frame of the anthropologist. The access to the field immediately activates a full participation. The researcher becomes an active member who has a clear function in a common artistic project where everybody participates.

Ethnotheatre promotes a more dialogic experience. Dialogical criticism — conceptualised by Bakhtin (1981) and appropriated by Conquergood (1985) — rests on two voices, two worldviews, and two systems of values and beliefs that can speak simultaneously and in interaction. Dialogue is an experience of being in the world. It is not exactly empathy. The idea is that both researcher and interlocutor question, debate, and challenge each other in an intensely committed dialogue. The anthropologist as ethnographer does not need to assume a definite and watertight position but instead host a space where ideologies are contested, a liminal space in which his persona and the participants of his research are together, even when they distance themselves apart from each other. As Conquergood (1985) says, it is a hyphen rather than a period.

The theatre director role potentially allows the access to data in surprising ways. In what concerns the process of inquiring, of interviewing, everyone ends up getting horizontally involved in the creative process, interacting through other frames, and completely re-configuring the ethnographic encounter. There is also a re-arrangement of how we collect data for the research. I will give you an example of the innumerable possible situations of doing it through dramatic play. I have done theatre with two different groups of inmates inside a prison. The first group is made of preventive detention inmates or pre-trial detention inmates and the second group has only convicted inmates serving their sentence.

One of the first exercises I undertook with these two groups as a form of understanding the group's cohesion was the following: the aim of the exercise is the self-counting of the participants in the room (there were twenty) in a focused way. Each person has to count himself once (in this case from one to twenty) and no one can speak simultaneously (when they do, the game is over).

When everybody got their turn, we reach the number of people in the room. Everybody has to be in some way connected so they do not overlap each other. The first group, the pre-trial ones, did not pass the number five. The second group, composed by convicted inmates, instantaneously, as I was explaining the rules of the game, arranged a form of doing it at the first attempt. They were in a circle and they agreed in a glimpse to tell the numbers from the left to the right (as coordinated by the alleged—and later confirmed—leader), so the person on the right would say the next number. I told them how surprised I was! Then I added another rule, they could not speak the numbers sequentially. Again, as I was creating this rule they already had a solution. The one on my right began, and then the one on my left said the next number, so the second one on my right would be the next, and so on.

This is one example of the explosion of data appearing without the need of asking. And it happened in the first session. The difference between the first and the second group was that the first one did not have any leader yet, they were improvising. In the second group, without asking, I knew who the leaders were because they were controlling the improvisation process, and immediately I was ready to start studying this dimension of the group without the need of asking about it. I confirmed with the social worker, who followed administratively the project, that they were the leaders. This is a mode of accessing the metacommunicative repertoire. The ethnographic encounter emerges from the *collective effervescence* (as Durkheim would say it) or the *communitas* (as Turner would reply) (Olaveson, 2001) that is provided by the practice of dramatic play. The environment of the ethnographic encounter reconfigures itself in a ludic manner. Within this environment, there is freedom to access hidden transcripts (Scott, 1990). This may happen in an improvisation as well as in the commentary phase elicited after any improvisation, in which everyone analyses what happened on stage.

In a third group of inmates I am now working with, we are watching the series *Orange is the New Black* based on the book by Piper Kerman (2011) and adapted for TV in 2013 by Jenji Kohan, Sara Hess and Tara Herrmann. We are doing it in order to get inspiration to make our own play about the life cycle or passage in the prison, since day one to the fulfilment of the punishment. The inmates are also aware of the credentialed expert but they keep framing me as a kind of teacher or performer, eroding the previous research role. Because we are doing an adaptation, here and there, they spontaneously talk about the vernacular reality. Things happening in the TV series trigger the revelation of ethnographic data, such as the use of slang vocabulary that allows me to make a vernacular dictionary; or a comment about the local parallel economy in the prison; or the sudden justification of why the cells sometimes burn on Wednesdays. Every Thursday, the things inmates requested to buy two days earlier arrive, meaning that they will be able to pay their debts, if they have them, with those groceries or cigarettes. When they accumulate many debts and cannot pay, the most famous and radical way out is to burn the cell and so wait for immediate transfer out of that wing—the prison has four wings). I have also always elicited themes, spaces, or scenes that I found inspiring for the play and that I can use as a tool to interview about such dimension of living in a prison. These are examples of hidden transcripts (Scott, 1990), which inmates use to communicate without the guards knowing (or can prevent), what I like to call as decentred marginality (Salgado, 2014). Persisting on a logic of exteriority to the centre, it detaches from the logic of the centre it criticises. This procedure may serve as the basis for an off-stage creative and productive resistance.

In each methodology of improvisation or theatrical construction that we put in action during the devised theatre, we may frame the moment with an exercise with its own rules, a dramatic play. We can direct this exercise towards any characteristic or dimension of the community we are dealing with. In a prison, we may make improvisations about the yard, or the systems of oppression life imprints on their life. Here, specific themes or universes of meaning will emerge freely for everybody to deal with. Other themes concerning their passage through the confinement emerge while performing or rehearsing. A process of collecting relevant data to dramatise in a rich and collaborative environment is constructed. For each situation, everybody has to clarify the subtexts and references that convey meaning to the dramaturgy.

We revolutionise the interview because we easily access the techniques and the local metacommunicative repertoire. This awareness of the native metacommunicative routines (speech, including nonverbal communication) can provide rich data and will suggest topics that can be further explored for analysis, as Briggs (1986) argued. Because they are extremely subtle, we need a sensitive performative quality of researching as well as a good form of documentation. Some information can only be conceptualised as metacommunicative sometime further in the research.

The contamination between artistic methodologies and ethnography puzzles the play of the roles that compose the research persona. This contamination also amplifies the possibilities of ethnographic recording modes. In the ethnotheatre mode of research, the documentation process may also unveil new material, activating practices and processes that open access to new ethnographic data. The recording modes replicate because:

a) We can take notes during the sessions or rehearsals without the problem of revealing what is important or not to the interlocutor. Once, in a session, an inmate asked me, "One day I would love to find out what you are writing in that notebook!". I immediately told him I was taking notes for the dramaturgy and so showed him (I offered notebooks and pens for that matter in the first session). I now had the excuse to write any kind of data.

b) We can video record the rehearsal. In the context of my research, I found out that some inmates, when in detention and without sentence, are not comfortable with being in a film. The camera was a factor of exclusion so I stopped using it. Unlike then, in the group I am currently working with, this theme once came up and I realised that this particular group of inmates is willing to consider the use of video recording in the play, for the sake of art.

c) We can even make the interlocutors take notes about the work of others and then collectively discuss what everyone saw, felt, understood—making focus group.

d) We can, for example, photograph an improvisation and, later, with the same interlocutor, carry out an interview which we can record either with audio or video, using photo-elicitation. Or we can later give that photo to the protagonist and ask him to tell a story or make an improvisation based on that photograph. Finally, the group can comment the performance which we also can film, and so on.

Photo-elicitation allows fieldnotes to elicit, activate, and generate abundant and reflexive information. In the framework of ethnotheatre, the documentation assumes a new performativity, in which interviewer and interviewee reflect on the events they both witnessed, thus creating empathy materialised in a photograph. What I mean is that the environment created by ethnotheatre activates the creation of diverse devices for the collection of ethnographic data. Fieldnotes generate new fieldnotes, replicating the recording and documentation modes for future analysis.

## 4. Conclusion: art-based ethnography on the road as radical pedagogy

Art-based research brings some advantages to the pursuits of ethnography when combined with participant observation. Particularly ethnotheatre opens the space for new relations and processes of framing the encounter that would otherwise be difficult to achieve. After working on a genealogy for ethnotheatre, after relating the history of performance studies with performance art, we saw how ethnodramatic writing might shape the research features, relating differently with the archive and the repertoire.

Taking devised theatre in its wide definition, we then engendered a creative process that allows experiments on theatre methodologies, in order to question how they differently serve the ethnographic purpose. There is also a revolution in the process of inquiring. Data emerges from different devices because we are all building a theatre play. The research persona we may deal with configures different kinds of encounters with the participants of the project. We may combine this type of data collection with the traditional roles of complete observer or make formal interviews. There is also an amplification of the ethnographic modes of recording, in different media and in different moments. Fieldnotes may replicate in other fieldnotes, and the relation between the researcher roles and modes of registration increases in variety.

In ethnotheatre, as Bryant Alexander (2005) suggests, the participants are the ones who choose to maintain or break the dormant perception of the habitus. The performance of ethnography explores and interferes in how they can act to influence social consciousness in relation to problematic human conditions and acknowledge the mechanisms of control as well as of resistance. Thereby there is a component of radical pedagogy, contributing to put culture in motion in a consequent and active way. There is a reinforcement of the role of anthropology to participate in the clarification of the socio-cultural difference in the margins. Ethnotheatre stirs up all these questions, expanding the possibilities of the ethnographic method to a playful and creative action research. It gives back to everybody a common space to the implicit tenets of being in the world.

### References

Alexander, B., (2005) Performance ethnography: The reenacting and inciting of culture, in Denzin, N. and Lincoln, Y., (eds.) *The Sage handbook of qualitative Research*, London: Sage.

Bakhtin, M., (1981) *The dialogic imagination: Four essays*, Austin: University of Texas Press.

Bogart, A. and Landau, T., (2005) *The viewpoints book: A practical guide to viewpoints and composition*, New York: Theatre Communications Group.

Blumenfeld-Jones, D., (2008) Dance, choreography, and social science research, in Cole, A. and Knowles, G., (eds.) *Handbook of the arts in qualitative research: Perspectives, methodologies, examples, and issues*, Thousand Oaks, CA: Sage Press.

Boal, A., (2005) *Teatro do oprimido e outras poéticas políticas [Theatre of the oppressed and other political poetics]*, Rio de Janeiro: Editora Civilização Brasileira.

Brecht, B. (n.d) *Estudos sobre teatro: Para uma arte não-Aristotélica [Essays on theatre: For an non-Aristotelic art]*, Lisbon: Portugália.

Briggs, C., (1986) *Learning how to ask: A sociolinguistic appraisal of the role of the interview in social science research*, Cambridge: Cambridge University Press.

Butler, J., (1993) *Bodies that matter: On the discursive limits of 'sex'*, London: Routledge.

Conquergood, D., (1998) Beyond the text: Toward a performative cultural politics, in Dailey, S.J., (ed.) *The future of performance studies: Visions and revisions*, Annandale, VA: National Communication Association.

Conquergood, D., (1985) Performing as a moral act: Ethical dimensions of the ethnography of performance, *Literature in Performance*, 2(5):1-13.

Cunha, M., (2014) The ethnography of prisons and penal confinement, *Annual Review of Anthropology*, 43:217-233.

Denzin, N., (1997) *Interpretive ethnography: Ethnographic practices for the twenty-first century*, London: Sage.

Estalella, A. and Sánchez-Criado, T., (2015) Experimental collaborations: An invocation for the redistribution of social research, *Convergence: The International Journal of Research into New Media Technologies*, 21(3):301-305.

Finley, S., (2005) Arts-based inquiry: Performing revolutionary pedagogy, in Denzin, N. and Lincoln, Y., (eds.) *The Sage handbook of qualitative research*, London: Sage.

Frois, C., (2017) *Mulheres condenadas: Histórias de dentro da prisão [Convicted women: Stories from inside a prison]*, Lisbon: Tinta da China.

Gold, R., (2001) Roles in sociological field observations, in Bryman, A. (ed.), *Ethnography (Sage benchmarks in research methods, volume II)*, London: Sage.

Kerman, P., (2011) *Orange is the new black: My year in a women's prison*, New York: Spiegel and Grau.

Innes, C., (1972) *Erwin Piscator's political theatre: The development of modern German drama*, Cambridge: Cambridge University Press.

Lampe, E., (2002) Rachel Rosenthal creating her selves, in Zarrilli, P., (ed.) *Acting (re) considered: A theoretical and practical guide*, London: Routledge.

Langellier, K., (1999) Personal narrative, performance, performativity: Two or three things I know for sure, *Text and Performance Quarterly*, 19(2):125-144.

Lassiter, L., (2005) *The Chicago guide to collaborative ethnography*, Chicago: The University of Chicago Press.

Myerhoff, B., (1982) Life history among the elderly: Performance, visibility and remembering, in Ruby, J., (ed.) *A crack in the mirror: Reflective perspectives in anthropology*, Philadelphia: University of Pennsylvania Press.

Norris, S., (2016) Concepts in multimodal discourse analysis with examples from video conferencing, *Yearbook of the Poznań Linguistic Meeting*, 2:141-165.

Olaveson, T., (2001) Collective effervescence and communitas: Processual models of ritual and society in Emile Durkheim and Victor Turner, *Dialectical Anthropology*, 26:89-124.

Piscator, E., (1995) From basic principles of a theory of sociological drama (1929), in Drain, R., (ed.) *Twentieth-century theatre: A sourcebook*, London: Routledge.

Phelan, P., (1998) Introduction: The ends of performance, in Phelan, P. and Lane, J., (eds.) *The ends of performance*, New York: New York University Press.

Pollock, D., (1998) Performing writing, in Phelan, P. and Lane, J., (eds.) *The ends of performance*, New York: New York University Press.

Reed-Danahay, D., (1997) Introduction, in Reed-Danahay, D., (ed.) *Auto/ethnography: Rewriting the self and the social*, New York: Berg.

Rosaldo, R., (1993) *Culture and truth: The remaking of social analysis (With a new introduction)*, Boston: Beacon Press.

Ruby, J. (ed.), (1982) *A crack in the mirror: Reflexive perspectives in anthropology*, Philadelphia: University of Pennsylvania Press.

Saldaña, J., (2011) *Ethnotheatre: Research from page to stage*, Walnut Creek: Left Coast Press.

Salgado, R. S., (2016) A Persona do antropólogo na etnografia como ação: O jogo dos papéis, do registo e as metodologias teatrais [The persona of the anthropologist at the ethnography as action: The play of the roles, the documentation and the theatre methodologies], in Martins, H. and Paulo Mendes, P., (eds.) *Trabalho de campo: Envolvimento e experiências em antropología [Fieldwork: Involvement and experiences in anthropology]*, Lisbon: ICS, Social Sciences Press.

Salgado, R. S., (2014) The politics of the dramatic play: De-centered marginality as creative resistance. *Mantichora*, 4(December): 11-22.

Salgado, R. S., (2013) Etnoteatro como performance da etnografia: Estudo de caso num grupo de teatro universitário [Ethnotheatre as performance of ethnography: A case study with university theatre group], *Cadernos de Arte e Antropologia*, 2(1):31-52.

Salgado, R. S., (2007) *State of exception. CITAC: An ethnohistorical project (1956-1978)*, Video: www.youtube.com/watch?v=kPnFpvBm9dw.

Schechner, R., (2015) *Performed Imaginaries*, London and New York: Routledge.

Scott, J. C., (1990) *Domination and the arts of resistance: Hidden transcripts*, New Haven, CT: Yale University Press.

Snow, D., Benford, R. and Anderson, L., (2001) Fieldwork roles and informational yield: A comparison of alternative settings and roles, in Bryman, A., (ed.) *Ethnography (Sage benchmarks in research methods, volume II)*, London: Sage Publications.

Spry, T., (2001) Performing autoethnography: An embodied methodological praxis, *Qualitative Inquiry*, 7(6):706-732.

Strathern, M., (1987) The limits of auto-anthropology, in Jackson, A. (ed.), *Anthropology at home (ASA Monographs 25)*, London: Tavistock Publications.

Taylor, D. (2007) *The archive and the repertoire: Performing cultural memory in the Americas*, Durham, NC: Duke University Press

Turner, V. and Turner, E., (1982) Performing ethnography, *The Drama Review*, 26(2):33-50.

Vasques, E., (2007) *Piscator e o conceito de 'Teatro épico' [Piscator and the concept of 'Epic theatre']*, Lisbon: Biblioteca da Escola Superior de Teatro e Cinema.

Chapter 7

# The Hat, the *Cobra*, and the
# Manchester Improv Collective

*Geoff Bright and Anton Hunter*

The Manchester Improv Collective (MIC) is an *improv* collective which runs a free-improv night in Manchester. The basic premise is that anyone can turn up and join in by putting their name in the hat. Names are pulled out, ensembles formed, and hearts broken. *From MIC web page.*

This chapter arises from an ethnographic study that we (Bright and Hunter) carried out in 2016-17 as part of a large EU funded research project: *Partispace: A Study of the Styles and Spaces of Young People's Participation across Eight European Cities (2015-18)*. The central research question of *Partispace* addressed how people under thirty years-old participate differently across social milieus, educational settings, and youth cultural scenes. As part of the research, a series of ethnographic studies have taken place. Here, we address one such study, which focuses on a vibrant music scene curated by the *Manchester Improv Collective* (MIC). MIC brings together a mobile and varying intergenerational group of amateur and professional musicians involved in monthly free improvisation nights (see Bailey, 1994 on improvisation generally, and Barre, 2014 and 2016; and Corbett, 2016, on UK *free* improvisation specifically). Characterised by non-hierarchical relationships and an egalitarian approach, MIC evenings are generally made up of a mix of random performance groupings (names are literally pulled out of a hat) and pre-scheduled improv performances. MIC also organises reasonably frequent musician workshops and has released albums on its own artist-centric record label.

For the purposes of this discussion, we focus in particular on how MIC's performance culture and practice might be productively understood in terms of a *social aesthetics* of improvisation (Born, Lewis and Straw, 2017). Concentrating particularly on participants under thirty years-old, we consider how what Born, Lewis and Straw have described as *empractice* (detailed below) shows up in the contrasting settings of three different playing formats observed at MIC: in the usual out-of-the-hat format adopted at monthly sessions; in three preparatory workshop sessions related to a public performance of John Zorn's large-scale improvisation *game* piece, *Cobra*; and in a subsequent public performance of the Zorn piece.

## 1. Background to the ethnographic case study

Manchester, like each of the other seven cities involved in *Partispace*, (Bologna, Eskişehir, Frankfurt, Gothenburg, Plovdiv, Rennes, and Zurich) was required to establish a series of six ethnographic case studies, and these were duly set up by a team of colleagues based at Manchester Metropolitan University and the University of Huddersfield. Studies across a range of Manchester area sites including youth groups, a political study group, a homelessness support group for men, a youth representational group, an on-line feminist group were established during early 2016 and the MIC study followed in the autumn of 2016. Initially, we were hesitant about the study, as MIC participants were generally at least at the very upper end of the *Partispace* age range of thirty years-old. Nevertheless, the site offered a distinctive setting that strengthened our team's city-wide response to the *Partispace* brief of attending to a *variety* of the styles, spaces and forms of participation. There was another key reason for going ahead with the MIC study, too. Musicians around MIC had been featured prominently in an article in *Wire*, the main UK experimental music magazine, in May 2016 (see Spicer, 2016) and the article deployed some then increasingly common *second city* tropes about the relationship and potentially positive and negative tensions that existed between Manchester—then being posed as a *Northern powerhouse*—and London. This narrative was present around other possible Manchester cases as well: an aspect that helped highlight the potential interest of the MIC case and suggested a relation to the other Manchester studies which had not at first been obvious.

## 2. Ethnographic approach

> The question posed is, how well are we equipped [to] ... capture the sensuous array of sights, sounds, and smells as well as represent the traumas, passions and emotions, of twenty-first century lived experiences? Such a challenge arguably calls for a re-working or shifting of ethnographic methodological boundaries     (Bagley, 2009: 251).

In this quotation, Carl Bagley issues a sharp challenge that is particularly pertinent to ethnographic studies of arts practice settings where the *sensuous array* is primary and, as co-producers, we have tried to respond to that in our general approach. We would emphasise, in particular, the complementary nature of the different but related expertise that we have brought to the study. Hunter, as performer and pedagogue, initially became involved in the project through his role as co-founder of MIC. His doctoral research, a *Practice as research-based enquiry into composing for large groups of improvising musicians*, looks specifically at how to include musicians in the creative act of composing in ways that might not usually happen. Bringing this experience and knowledge to the *Partispace* project deepened the study of the different settings that we intended to observe, placing some of the activity in a wider context related to the history of free improvisation, as well as providing the music pedagogy skills needed to run the workshops. The work that Bright as ethnographer and performer has brought together in the recent period has tried to respond in general terms to Bagley's plea by emphasising the fruitfulness of two particular ethnographic approaches: Sarah Pink's work on sensory ethnography (Pink, 2009) and Kathleen Stewart's (2007) approach to the contingent *worlding* of what she calls *ordinary affects*. Pink, highlighting the *sensorium and arts practice* (Pink, 2009: 8) emphasises how a sensorial turn to 'multisensoriality is integral both to the lives of people who participate in our research *and* to how we ethnographers practice our craft' (Pink, 2009: 1). Stewart, on the other hand, takes us into an ethnographic territory where affects flow and intensify as they

> … accrue, endure, fade or snap. How they build as a refrain, literally scoring over the labour of living out whatever's happening. How they constitute a compositional present, pushing circulating forces into form, texture and density so that can be felt, imagined, brought to bear or just born.                                                    (Stewart, 2010: 2).

Such a distinctive form of affective ethnographic attention, and the vocabulary it deploys, is ideally suited to the free-form improvised music considered here.

We also note how our project design grew organically out of a conversation that we had already begun about potential applications of critical improvisation studies (see Lewis and Piekut, 2016) in fields beyond music: in, for example, education, community development and, with particular relevance to *Partispace*, youth support (see Harris, 2014). Our core idea was that our relationship as players—initially established through a third-party musician with whom we both played regularly, but independently of each other—might be put to work by us in using improvisation's dialogic form as a relational reflexive medium within our ethnographic study. Consequently, our working relationship has essentially been conceived as a duo (in an improvisational sense): Hunter would take a participation observation role as MIC co-curator, musician, and workshop leader, while Bright occupied a performance ethnography role as ethnographer and musician. We would thus experiment with a research practice modelled on improvised performance protocols (Soules, 2004) whereby a bi-directional flow of connectivity might be established between the performance aspects of the project and the more conventional ethnographic practices involved in gathering observations and developing an interpretive frame. This approach, we both feel, has in fact been a productive feature of the project, and our writing relationship has progressed as much through a spirit of spontaneous interaction as it has as a conventional authorial collaboration.

In summary, our collaborative performance approach has enabled a particular, dual attentiveness to the participative practice encouraged by MIC and has been instrumental in us offering a social aesthetic account of what we are tentatively calling *flows of relational intensity* around different dimensions of player inexperience/experience; the changing status of performance from rehearsal to performance; and the political/aesthetic character of improvisational interaction.

### 3. Social Aesthetics

Social Aesthetics (SA) (see Born, Lewis and Straw, 2017) is part of a strengthening renewal of interest in the relationship between politics, aesthetics and ethics in arts practice—particularly as that relationship touches on improvisation—that is taking a number of very interesting directions (see, as examples, McMullen, 2016, on *the improvisative*, and LaBelle, 2108, on *sonic agency*). Critiquing the relational aesthetics of Bourriaud (see Born, 2017) and at the same time picking up the politicised approach of such as Kester (2004), the core of SA is a 'rejection of the claim, however grounded, that one can or should disentangle the social, in all its varied modalities, from experiences and conceptions of the aesthetic' (Born, Lewis and Straw, 2017: 2). Indeed, 'just as social (and economic and political) conditions and processes shape art and music, so do art and music shape social (and economic and political) life' (2017: 6). Born, Lewis and Straw push even further, however, arguing that the aesthetic and the social are not only contingently co-productive but are, in fact, immanently related. Art, musical and performance practices are *immanently social* and can, in improvised performance, actually instantiate or, in the authors' term, *empractice* 'novel realms of social experience, *new modes of sociality*' (2017: 9, our emphasis). From an SA point of view, improvised performance then,

> ... *enacts an alternative to*, and embodies a critique and rejection of, the social relations ... constructed by the western art music tradition and is in this critical respect ... an act of social experimentation.
>
> (2017: 9, our emphasis)

Politicised approaches to theorising art practice are not new and have made a consistently dissident appearance in the philosophy of art and art practices since the 1950s. Basically, SA picks up on some of these threads but distinctively accentuates the prefigurative capacity of art and music 'to both influence social processes and to *put into practice, model, enact, and experiment* with novel socialities and social relations of diverse kinds' (2017: 6, our emphasis). Here, then, we have a working definition of *empractice*: as the distinctive mode of social/aesthetic relationality whereby improvisation's immanence is materialised through a micro-politics of performance. According to the account given by Born, Lewis and Straw, improvisation '*cannot but empractice* or manifest a social aesthetics' (our emphasis) as a world otherwise than the formal, hierarchical spaces of the music academy/*conservatoire*, and the generally competitive field of professional musicianship. We will have a look at how this account fits against the lived practices of participants in MIC in the discussion below. In the meantime, it will be useful to hold the concept of *empractice* closely in mind. For the moment, however, let us return to the ethnographic details of the MIC community.

## 4. The MIC community

The monthly MIC sessions that we observed and participated in all took place in the regular performance space in the upstairs room at *F Café* in Manchester. Now in its tenth year, The MIC is well known on the improv circuit and has a solid reputation. As well as the monthly sessions, there is a wider MIC network in which some key figures are consistently significant, while others come and go. This wider network has links to other scenes across the North West of England and, for a period, MIC had a twin session across the Pennines in Sheffield. In terms of musician biographies, MIC is both related to, and distinct from, other Manchester/NW jazz and improv scenes (and the conservatoire).

Certain figures—co-author Hunter, C, and B—(names have been anonymised and abbreviated) appear again and again in conversations with participants and in interviews that are part of our data. The MIC format of open, randomised improvisation sessions with pre-booked *featured performer* slots provides playing space for local, regional, national and international artists (the latter often as part of a small UK tour that usually involves a beginning or end gig in London). MIC's declared objective is to support and network improvised music: 'we aim to make [MIC] a staple in the improvisation scene by continuing to re-imagine what it can be, and how it can best serve musicians and artists both locally, and abroad' (MIC webpage).

In general, participants bring different levels of practical competence, musical and historical knowledge and training to their involvement in MIC and enter and settle within the community in different ways. As was clear from observation and conversations at MIC, accomplished players might be as frequently self-taught as they might be conservatoire trained. Irrespective of background, some (W for example) prioritise themselves as part of a politicised DIY scene, while others (T for example) function as professional players playing in a number of settings as their music careers develop. In general, both groups see MIC as an essential support for their musicianship.

Demographics within the small community are interesting. During the case study, the actual group of participants in MIC was made up of predominantly two age groupings: those under, around and just over thirty years-old and those in their fifties and sixties. This distribution probably speaks to two moments (see Barre, 2014, and Toop, 2016) within the music—the early 1970s and the recent period of the last ten years or so—and also to two overlapping approaches: as a politicised DIY culture, or as part of a modernist aesthetic of the avant-garde (Prévost, 1995, is informative on the impact of these distinctions). Additionally, the last twenty years or so have seen free improvisation become much more acceptable as a technical supplement to more conventional training within the music academy (which is very strong in Manchester) and there was evidence that this *top up* aspect played a role for three professional musicians that we spoke to at length (O, T and W). In gender terms, participation at MIC during the project observations was always predominantly men, with perhaps twenty per cent of *ad hoc* performers being women with the number rising to around forty per cent of *featured artists*. This lack of gender balance is still a notoriously common inequity in jazz (as the national and international literature shows—see *Committee on the Status of Women*, 2002; Maus, 2011; Whyton and Bruckner-Haring, 2013) *and* in improv, as our experience as players attests. Further—but, in this, *unlike* the jazz scene—ethnicity was almost exclusively white. These demographics, while not the direct focus of our attention here, do sit uncomfortably with an approach like Social Aesthetics, and we will flag them again in our concluding remarks.

During the preliminary discussions and first field visits, interesting aspects of the relationship between musicians and how their participation seemed to flow around certain thresholds, caught our eye. Visible groupings could be described very roughly as *casual improvisers, advanced students* and *giggers,* with accomplishment in the form being distributed generally (but with exceptions) from less experienced to more experienced across that same spectrum. The thresholds noticed were, first, at *entry* to the scene for new players; secondly, at the point where already accomplished young players become *positioned as candidates for participation in fee earning* and touring bands as *giggers* with a portfolio career commonly involving mixed genre performance, recording and instrumental teaching; and, thirdly, at differential levels of performance intensity experienced in informal out-of-the-hat playing, in the more formal space of a *performance,* and at the high point of being a *featured artist.* It was in an attempt to amplify these discernible differences and see how they impacted on performance that we decided, firstly, to supplement the standard *ad hoc and featured artist* approach of MIC with a public *mini festival* (and associated workshops) that we called the *MICstival* and, secondly, to organise our empirical materials in relation to intensities of *empractice* as differently constituted through these varied performance spaces.

## 5. A *loose network* harking back to the *loft* movement?

Arrived at *F Café* not far off eight o'clock and surprised to find H already there and the guys from the featured duo setting up wind instruments and electronic manipulation. Gorgeous sound when warming up. Wind playing to laptop. Not sure how the processing is working—some interesting lighting effects from small blue tubes like UV light ... operated in sync somehow with the laptop. Electronics on small plinth and laptop hand controlled through *handlebars* that he shakes, oscillates. H relaxed, easy, tells me about his injured thumb (walked into a wall!) and the forthcoming gig at Brighton Alternative Music Festival this coming weekend. I notice how the anecdote creates a feeling for me of being an insider to the pro gig network. It's the usual set up with bands. By the time we get started (nearer nine o'clock) there are a good few players in tonight ... a number who were here in August, but others too. A small group *checking things out* seem to know people who know people. Music college? Gigs? Conversations about 'bring instruments next time'.

(Bright, field notes)

MIC is very emphatically established upstairs at *F Café* and has been, with only a few associated events happening elsewhere, since its inception: a spatial configuration that Hunter retrospectively recognises as a happy (half) accident that conjures the 1970s New York *loft* movement (see Heller, 2017). The fact that MIC takes place in the upper room determines the feel of participation in a number of obvious ways. The performance room is upstairs which hampers large instruments somewhat. It doesn't have a bar (so this is not a drinking night in any real sense) but the ambience is explicitly Boho, DIY and participatory. Also, like the loft movement, which used cheap rent in *undesirable* areas (Heller, 2017: 26-30) to promote improvised music and a variety of other non-mainstream activities, *F Café* will not allow an entrance charge to be made. Again, this serves to position the monthly sessions in a certain way.

The performance space is small and quickly feels full if more than fifteen or so people are present. Just a small gathering feels very concentrated and lively, and the playing space with anything more than a quartet is cramped for players. *F Café* itself is a busy vegetarian café with a clientele of couples and mixed small groups of people mainly under thirty-five years-old. Heller has noted how in the loft movement 'networks materialised with clear connections to certain types of physical space' (2017: 122-123) but has also reflected that while 'the lofts promoted a high degree of freedom for individual artists, a lack of external engagement made it impractical as a strategy for mounting effective social critique' (2017: 92). In one of our research conversations as the project developed, Hunter introduced a similarity and a difference around Heller's point: "I think there's another link here with MIC. Although we don't position ourselves explicitly as trying to mount any kind of social critique, I think it's certainly true that what happens in our little bubble does struggle to impact on much outside of that. I rarely see regulars at other improvised music concerts in Manchester for example, although T. [one of our interviewees] is a notable exception to that".

While explicit *social critique* might be eschewed, MIC *is* defined in its web page mission statement as a *collective* which, like the tongue in cheek webpage reference to MIC being a somewhat dangerous place for reputations, signals the egalitarianism of MIC's approach to free-improv. In our observation—and supported by ethnographic interview with participants—there is a genuinely benevolent inclusiveness around MIC, whereby everyone is accepted as participating on their own terms and without pressure, and new participants are welcome simply as *someone new*. The web page acts as a key statement of the role of MIC, detailing links and still highlighting how the MIC record label which ran from 2009-2012 was based on an *artist first* model which gave profits to the artists and used an in-house recording/engineering team and art/graphic design team to take artists 'from idea to physical release in their hand, all for free'.

While there is a sense of the MIC sessions being a part of an established improvising world that reaches back to the 1960s and extends internationally, we are both weary and wary of the notion of a *scene* in relation to MIC or of any kind of Manchester-based upsurge of musical innovation. Hunter specifically feels that the *Wire* article referred to above is an example of how *scenes* are conjured around other stories that are seen as newsworthy—in this case around the balance of power between London and a northern counterweight in Manchester. A loose *network*, rather than a scene would, we suggest, be a much more accurate way of describing the relationship of the group of MIC players who share a commitment to free improv for at least part of their playing time. Three portfolio professional musician/teacher/composers that we spoke to in depth actually come and go in terms of their participation at MIC, and their affiliation reduces or intensifies in relation to the demands and availability of their paid work. These musicians reported their reasons for participation as a mix of socialising, recreation, and an opportunity for musical challenge in a satisfying musical form that has the virtue of *not* requiring rehearsal or familiarisation time.

### 6. : Out of a hat

According to participants, they use the randomised *out of the hat* performance sessions to develop their improvisation and listening skills in playing with differently experienced players in situations that are completely freely improvised and where instrumentation is often unusually clustered (there may be three guitars, or no guitars in any trio, for example). Further, the random group setting is generally regarded as a very low pressure, informal one where, from our point of view, the social dimension of *empractice* generally tends to dominate the aesthetic. In their own testimony, participants use the sessions to *chill*, hear who's doing what and where, check out new players and scope out potential collaborations. Thus, the randomised bands are a key aspect of how MIC supports the developing gig experience of players who are either early professionals or aspiring professionals specialising in improvised and other music forms. The period of years between twenty-five to thirty years -old appears to be decisive in the formation (or not) of a musician's professional playing career, and we note the immediate mutual recognition and networking of the players who *can play* ("we'll have to get you over to Sheffield", "I enjoyed your set") and are struck by how this happens without causing any apparent discomfort between players of one status or another, from near beginners to highly accomplished players.

All of these primarily social characteristics do not militate against aesthetic elements, however, and the co-constitutive power of both the social and the aesthetic seems well balanced in these often quite low-key, ad-hoc groupings. Even so, participants are visibly excited and animated when there has clearly been significant and meaningful interaction. They will comment enthusiastically to each other after the session is over, and a conversation may be initiated about *getting together*. As one would expect, different groupings are differently productive in aesthetic terms but the performers seem not to be exercised by this, moving happily back into networking as soon as they put their instruments down. Meanwhile, while all sessions are warmly and courteously greeted by the audience (largely the players who, at that moment, are not playing), the more aesthetically developed performances do get applauded more enthusiastically, which seems to be something of a paradox. These rapid movements and reversals notwithstanding, the out of the hat sessions are clearly highly productive in establishing a fundamentally social aesthetic practice. The situations observed in the preparatory *Cobra* workshops and actual *MICstival* performances are more complex, with pedagogic norms in the former and the intensity of public performance in the latter, being influential.

### 7. *Empractice*: Workshopping *Cobra*

First a few words about *Cobra*. *Cobra*, one of John Zorn's *game pieces* composed in 1984, is his 'most popular and well-known composition.' (Brackett, 2010: 44). In it, he directs his carefully selected ensemble using a series of cue cards and prompts to define who is playing and the manner in which they interact with each other, but not precisely what they play. By not publishing the score (such as it is) or instructions, Zorn has sought to ensure that the piece can only be performed when he is directly involved and has assembled the musicians he has chosen. Discussing the possibility of rotating the role of prompter for the piece, Zorn has said that he experimented with this in early performances, but that 'ultimately, I'm the best prompter there can be, because then I can be a complete fascist!' (Brackett, 2010: 50), a somewhat bizarre (comic?) statement that resonates with Born's appraisal of the *game pieces* as 'a kind of parodic authoritarian staging of controlled social encounters modelled on sports or war games.' (Born, 2017: 49)

Disregarding Zorn's emphatic ownership of *Cobra*, others have compiled a list of his rules and cue cards, and the piece is a widely used and powerful workshop piece which tends to get chosen largely due to the lack of any prescribed ideas about what or how each musician should play. As such, it is ideal for an improvising community such as that MIC and also, crucially, doesn't exclude anyone from professional or amateur backgrounds because everyone is free to play their instrument within the limits of their own abilities. Framing *Cobra* in relation to 'four planes of social mediation', Born has described it as relating to the first plane, that of the 'microsocialities of improvised performance' (Born, 2017: 48)

> ... conveying both how the orchestration of these socialities is taken to be immanent in performance aesthetics and how the same microsocialities are conceived of reflexively as a locus of experimentation. (Born, 2017: 48)

In the run-up to the *MICstival*, Hunter facilitated two workshop sessions on *Cobra* that took place at Manchester Metropolitan University and Bright, as a performer ethnographer, was involved as a participant performer in each one. Each workshop attracted around twenty participants, most of whom were under thirty years-old, most of whom stayed with the project through to the final workshop and performance on the day of the *MICstival*, and two or three of whom were MIC regulars. A large proportion of the group were students from the Royal Northern College of Music, with two travelling from Leeds College of Music.

Workshopping of *Cobra* requires considerable attention to the compositional use of the capacities of a *scratch* band and the highly structured *Cobra* form. Similarly, there is a need to manage the tension between participating performers *following instructions* and *listening* because of the rapidly changing nature of a *Cobra* performance. A noticeable feature of the workshops related to how Hunter and the participants adapted almost immediately to a recognisably *pedagogic workshopping* practice that has brought historically non-mainstream approaches (free improvisation, for example) into the mainstream of music teaching and learning. For example, the horseshoe layout of the workshop room (a university theatre space) just seemed to flow *naturally* out of the random seating arrangement that the group met on arrival and into a *workshop space*, as everyone read the space as a familiar one. Another noticeable feature was that the players who were also regular at the usual MIC sessions quickly became pro-active in the rule governed interaction/exchange aspects of *Cobra*. T for example—who formerly led an experimental *contemporary classical* workshop band at university—became a lead in shaping the in-the-moment compositional development of the pieces being produced. Basically, instructional and ensemble leadership roles seemed to come out of nowhere very quickly. The workshop sessions, then, seemed significantly less able to approach *empractice*, due (probably not surprisingly) to the conventionalised socialities of teaching and learning in music education. The *MICstival* however, seemed to occupy a space somewhere midway between the out of the hat and the workshop sessions.

## 8. *Empractice*: the *MICstival*

The *MICstival* took place on an afternoon and evening in January, 2017, at the usual venue and was built around a third workshop session of Zorn's *Cobra* in the afternoon, an evening session of *featured artist* performances, and a final performance of *Cobra* by the *workshop band*. The most obvious observable aspect of the *MICstival* was a universal intensification of participation which, while it varied between individuals and groupings across the spectrum of the workshop band, its conductors, and the featured performer bands, nevertheless suggested a default towards control (and away from *empractice*). Among the workshoppers, there was an immediately noticeable intensification of concentration that was palpable and seemed to be something to do with the fact that direction had now been taken over by C, rather than Hunter, who had run the two previous workshops at MMU.

Interestingly, a running joke about how C had missed a workshop due to a rescheduled flight made itself present in the *Cobra* performance, where it became material for one of the conducted parts and played a key role in the extent to which the *Cobra* performance instantiated *empractice*. Working a potential tension between the two directors, C's conducting cleverly incorporated a kind of *faux* rant on Hunter's behalf at the way that C was doing things, and that injected an uncertainty ("is this real, or is it part of the performance?") into the event. This instantaneous device was not only socially and aesthetically intelligent within the scope of *Cobra*'s particular form, but also served, through a playful moment of *who is in charge?*, to performatively challenge MIC's horizontal social aesthetic at the same time as it invited it back into the performance equation. In doing so, it immediately reconstituted the performance as *empractice* in SA terms.

At a more mundane level, significant changes in the way individual players participated in the intensified setting of a *public* performance were visible and pushed in the other direction. T who had quickly established himself as a key figure in the workshop group, was visible again as a participant who was keen to actively shape spontaneous compositions. A professional musician with a lot of experience in workshop facilitation and used to *professional* standards of performance, the change in his comportment and demeanour was very striking and in significant contrast to his approach in the out-of-the-hat sessions where his contribution had been characterised by a considered minimalism and reflectiveness.

## 9. Conclusion

In concluding, we would like to cluster our observations in two areas. Our primary focus here has been on immediate performance contexts and the way different formats affect the realisation (or not) of *empractice* in complicated ways. A secondary concluding focus—limited by space but certainly no less important—has intruded by necessity and calls on us to re-iterate our already mentioned concern at how the continuing problem of a lack of diversity in jazz and related forms like free improv in fact militates against the growth of politicised practices of improvisation.

To sum up our first points: our ethnographic presence consistently registered how the quality of improvisatory attention and practice tended to shift as the MIC participants (at all levels of experience) moved from the informally productive and definite *empractice* of the regular ad-hoc groupings (MIC's staple format), to the stable but conventional pedagogic relationships of the *Cobra* workshops, and on to the unstable intermediate aesthetic sociality of the final performances. We saw participant performers move through these sometimes risky, sometimes reassuring, flows in a variety of personal ways, but within a broadly collective logic. That is, every performer tended to flow the same way in a given performance context: towards collective production in the out-of-the-hat scenario; towards individual learning in the workshops; and towards a refined balance of the aesthetic and the social (characterised by heightened attention and accelerated responses) in the public performances. The most important advantage of using a social aesthetic perspective to think through these materials is that it allows us to move away from generalised psychological conventionalities about the links between increasing formality of performance and reduction of competence due to anxiety, and focus instead on improvisation as a much more sophisticated and complex relationality that is achieved to different degrees in different performance contexts such as those deliberately encouraged at MIC, and that has much to offer outside and beyond music contexts. We can then get on with the important job of replicating and extending such spaces—which will be all to the good.

In respect of the wider social context of improvised music, however, our secondary conclusion is less positive. We can still hear a jarring note around diversity. Aspects of the MIC case study point to structures of gender, race and class that remain persistently exclusive in music. As the literature shows, a gender imbalance is still pretty much universal across UK performance scenes related to jazz (Whyton and Bruckner-Haring, 2013), notwithstanding the established authority of Feminist approaches to cultures of music and the high level of awareness of the specific experiences of women musicians that is now being achieved (see Hannaford, 2017). Consequently, it remains difficult to eradicate such an imbalance even in the proactively egalitarian setting of MIC. As we would evidence from our own performance experience, ethnic uniformity is also a prominent feature in UK improv circles (at least outside London) which we would speculatively suggest is an aspect of the complex relationship of improv, on the one hand, to jazz (and *free jazz* in particular) as a Black music and, on the other, to a predominantly white *Conservatoire*. Class is less obvious, being somewhat hidden in plain sight in improvised music. There is evidence from our observation that the group of regular performers at MIC is quite mixed in social class terms, but the mix tends to be across another dimension of improv: to the *conservatoire* (again) but this time as predominantly middle class, and to popular forms such as punk and rock on the other.

Obviously, these demographic features relate to societal inequities, but they are also reproduced through the different genealogies that we noticed earlier as feeding into improvised music. While our interviews and research conversations at MIC frequently indicate a refreshing generational tilt away from (often masculinised) virtuosity towards the politicised world-making aspects of improvisation emphasised in MIC's horizontal experimentalism and in social aesthetics, it is still not easy to see how social aesthetic practices of improvisation can truly flourish on anything more than a small scale, or be credibly argued as potentially transformational in cognate fields, while such structural barriers remain in place.

## References

Bagley, C., (2009) Guest editorial: Shifting boundaries in ethnographic methodology, *Ethnography and Education*, 4(3):251-254.

Bailey, D., (1992) *Improvisation: Its nature and practice in music*, London: The British Library

Balliger, R., (1995) Sounds of resistance, in Sakolsky, R. and Wei-han Ho, F., (eds.) *Sounding off! Music as subversion / resistance / revolution*, Brooklyn: Autonomedia.

Barre, T., (2014) *Beyond jazz: Plink, plonk and scratch, The golden age of free music in London* 1966-72, Brentford: Compass Press

Barre, T., (2017) *Convergences, divergences and affinities: The second wave of free improvisation in England, 1973-79*, Brentford: Compass Press.

Born, G., (2017) After Relational Aesthetics: Improvised music, the social, and (re)theorizing the aesthetic, in Born, G., Lewis, E. and Straw, W., (eds.) *Improvisation and social aesthetics*, Durham, North Carolina: Duke University Press.

Born, G., Lewis, E. and Straw, W., (2017) *Improvisation and social aesthetics*, Durham, North Carolina: Duke University Press.

Brackett, J., (2010) Some notes on John Zorn's *Cobra*, *American Music, 28*(1):44-75.

Committee on the Status of Women (2002), *Bibliography of sources related to women's studies, gender studies, feminism, and music*, Stanford: Society for Music Theory https://ccrma.stanford.edu/~leigh/csw/csw/CSWBib2.html [Accessed 2 April 2018]

Corbett, J., (2016) *A listener's guide to free improvisation*, Chicago: University of Chicago Press.

Denzin, N., (2003) *Performance ethnography: Critical pedagogy and the politics of culture*, London: Sage.

Hannaford, M., (2017) Subjective (re)positioning in musical improvisation: Analysing the work of five female improvisers, *Music Theory Online*, 23(2):1-26.

Harris, P., (2014) The youth worker as jazz improviser: foregrounding education 'in the moment' within the professional development of youth workers, *Professional Development in Education,* 40(4):1-15

Heller, M., (2017) *Loft jazz: Improvising New York in the 1970s*, Oakland: University of California Press.

Kester, G., (2004) *Conversation pieces: Community and communication in modern art*, Berkeley: University of California Press.

LaBelle, B., (2018) *Sonic agency,* London: Goldsmiths Press

Lewis, G. and Piekut, B., (2016) *The Oxford handbook of critical improvisation studies, Volume 1*, Oxford, Oxford University Press.

Lewis, G. and Piekut, B., (2016) *The Oxford handbook of critical improvisation studies, Volume 2*, Oxford, Oxford University Press.

Maus, F., (2011) Music, gender, and sexuality, in Clayton, M., Herbert, T. and Middleton, R., (eds) *The cultural study of music: A critical introduction*, London and New York: Routledge,

McMullen, T., (2016) The imporovisative, in Lewis, G. and Piekut, B., (eds) *The Oxford handbook of critical improvisation studies, Volume 1*, Oxford, Oxford University Press.

Prévost, E., (1995) *No sound is innocent*, Harlow: Copula.

Pink, S., (2009) *Doing sensory ethnography*, London: Sage.

Soules, M., (2004) Improvising character: Jazz, the actor, and protocols of improvisation, in Fischlin, D. and Heble, A., (eds) *The other side of nowhere: Jazz, improvisation, and communities in dialogue*, Middletown, CT: Wesleyan University Press.

Spicer, D., (2016) Manchester's new improv underground, *The Wire,* 387:32-37.

Stewart, K., (2007) *Ordinary affects*, Durham, NC: Duke University Press.

Stewart, K., (2010) Atmospheric attunements, *Rubric*, 1:1-14.

Toop, D., (2016) *Into the maelstrom: Music, improvisation and the dream of freedom before 1970*, London: Bloomsbury

Whyton, T and Bruckner-Haring, C., (eds) (2013) *Statistical overview of five partner countries*, Graz: Institute for Jazz Research, University of Music and Performing Arts Graz.

## Chapter 8

# *Lost and found*: Ethnographic researcher and arts practitioners getting lost and coming home[1]

*Harriet Rowley*

The relationship between arts practitioners, researchers, youth and community workers, social workers and young men living vulnerable and unhoused lives in Manchester City Centre is a complex and enduring one, dating back to the establishment of *The Box* a decade ago. From research with *The Box*, a combined arts and social work charity for vulnerable young men, my colleague Batsleer (2011) explored the potential for arts-based practices to open up communicative possibilities including those of advocacy, mutual recognition and empowerment. She juxtaposes this against those often found in formal and informal education settings where efforts to enable student voice can be viewed as tokenistic and adult-led. Arnot and Reay (2007) identify how school-based settings are typically guilty of restricted notions of student voice. Batsleer (2011) uses this framework, influenced by Bernstein, to show how youth work also operates via pedagogic codes. She recognises that professional practice of youth workers thus tends to provoke identity talk that is structured by polarising discourses on the conditions of youth. Furthermore, whilst efforts to include marginalised groups within formal democratic structures have sought to include excluded groups, these can simultaneously entrench classifications and forms of symbolic violence to those who are not given access. Such practices mean that the scope of participation is limited whilst the extent that different groups of young people have to learn and experience modes of civic engagement threatens efforts to promote democracy. In contrast, arts-based strategies are positioned as having the potential to offer more inclusive and democratic modes of practice because of how they can cope with complexity, temporal relations and expression of feeling (Batsleer, 2011).

In educational research, the importance of student or pupil voice in relation to democratic schools has sought to provide a more inclusive and progressive alternative from the neo-liberal individual choice-based approach to education (Fielding, 2004; Wrigley, Thomson and Lingard, 2012). More broadly, within youth-based research in the field of sociology, the importance of the participation

1.  This project receives funding from the European Union's Horizon 2020 Research and Innovation Programme under Grant Agreement N°: 649416

of young people can be formally traced back to the *UN Convention on the Right of the Child* (Holland et al., 2010). Article 12 ratified that children have a right to have a say on matters, which concern their lives. Research on children's and young people's participation in social, civic and political processes has consequently grown whilst there has also been recognition that there is a need to co-produce knowledge and the potential benefits for those involved (Percy-Smith and Thomas, 2010). Traditional methods of data collection such as interviews and participant observation associated with ethnography that distance and reinforce power relations by positioning the researcher as expert and the young person as participant are less favoured, whilst arts-based methods such as theatre and visual methods have been utilised to try to democratise knowledge making (Thomson, 2008). Furthermore, in respect to marginalised groups, the extractive and intrusive nature of interviews as akin to oppressive practices used by the state as modes of surveillance have forced qualitative researchers to question their suitability (Enria, 2016; Sinhar and Back, 2014). Such ways of collecting data are seen to risk further objectification and can too easily reproduce representations, which are constructed on narratives of victimhood where the agency of participants is removed (Polkinghorne, 1996). In contrast, the use of multi-media and participatory approaches to data collection have the potential for participants to exert more control on how their lives are represented whilst the exchange which follows can enable sense-making which constitutes a sociable process of 'travelling alongside in dialogue' (Sinhar and Back, 2014; 484).

It is within this context that the project *Lost and Found* was constructed. This chapter describes how arts-based practices were utilised within a specific research project focused on exploring young people's participation and voice in an informal education setting. Firstly, I describe why *The Box* was chosen as a case study site and how access to the field site was negotiated. The research design is then outlined whilst particular attention is given to steps which were taken to deliberately speak to the aforementioned considerations within literature on young people's participation both in research and as a focus of study. Furthermore, the utilisation of arts-based practices and the process enacted in relation to an ethnographic approach is explored. To structure this discussion, I reflect upon five ways of using arts-based practices as identified by Batsleer (2011) to consider how symbolisation, expression of feeling, ownership, risk-taking and play were important to the execution and, in turn, the findings of *Lost and Found*. In this sense, I explore the communicative possibilities which were made possible as a consequence to art-based practices when used alongside ethnography which has implications for how young people's participation in research and as a focus of study can be understood. More broadly, this chapter thus contributes to debates concerned with issues of voice and representation of marginalised groups in terms of the possibilities and limits of creativity in enabling more inclusive democratic practice.

## 1. The fieldwork site

PARTISPACE (partispace.eu) is an EU funded Horizon 2020 project investigating spaces and styles of young people's participation across eight European cities. One of the case study cities is Manchester, UK in which a team of four academics, including myself, from Manchester Metropolitan University (MMU) formed a research team led by Janet Batsleer. The research project was funded from 2015 to 2018 whilst the majority of the empirical work took place during 2016/17. Six case study sites of young peoples' participation were selected in each of the eight cities, thus comprising of forty-eight cases in total. Due to our strong connections to the city where we live and work, we made a decision early on to connect our selection of case study sites to prevalent issues facing young people in Manchester.

On the European stage, the United Kingdom is currently notable for wanting to take action to leave the European Union. Rising inequality is recognised as a key factor, which influenced those who voted for Brexit, whilst at a local level the consequences of cuts to local authority budgets can be visibly seen on the streets in the form of increasing amounts of people who are homeless. As identified by John Healey, the former Shadow Secretary of State for Housing and Planning, the housing crisis was key in UK's decision to leave the EU, he argued:

> The gap between haves and have-nots was the breeding ground for Brexit, and these new figures today show that the number of homeless households has risen by an astonishing 54% since 2010.
>
> (The Independent, 2016)

In Manchester, the increase of those affected led to formation of *camps* where rows of tents occupied parts of the city, including one underneath the motorway in the university district. In 2015 when we were selecting the case study sites, MMU applied for an injunction so the police could forcibly remove the occupiers. As employees, we received an email reassuring us that the university and city council would endeavour to support 'genuine cases of homelessness.' Discourses of deservedness are frequent in neo-liberal framings of the homeless community yet some students and staff did attempt forms of solidarity by joining in protests (Figure 8.1). Such acts of participation are frequently delegitimised yet there is a concern across Europe that we are witnessing a crisis of representative democracy (Newton, 2011). PARTISPACE starts from the assumption that there is a relation between the apparent lack of participation among young people on the one hand, and the prevalence of ideological and discursive limitations of what is recognised as participation on the other.

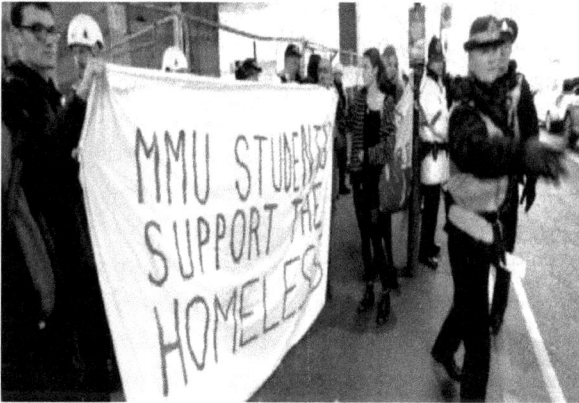

Figure 8.1: MMU staff and students protest against eviction of homeless camp in Manchester

In attempt to broaden the definition of what can be considered as participation as well as speak to current issues of voice and representation in the city, we selected *The Box* as one of the case study sites. Due to previous research (Batsleer, 2011), we were thus able to build on existing relationships and negotiate access with members of the homeless community in Manchester. The charity has existed in various guises since 2004, working with men aged eighteen to thirty years-old. Unlike the majority of other charities providing support to the homeless community in the city, participation in *The Box* involves an interesting combination of creative engagement and access to health and social care support.

## 2. Charting the process of *Lost and Found*

In May 2015, I began nine months of ethnographic fieldwork, spending two to three evenings a week carrying out participant observation on the streets and different community settings where workers from *The Box* target their work.

Janet Batsleer's prior involvement with *The Box* meant that a strong relationship existed between her and John Doyle, the Creative Director who led the program of work, and she acted as important gatekeeper in ensuring there would be a good fit between my skills and the needs of the organisation. From the beginning, through meetings between Janet, John and myself, we envisioned that I would not be a distant bystander researcher but would co-facilitate a project that would combine the research aims of PARTISPACE with arts-based practices. Above all, we were conscious of the aforementioned literature concerned with young people's participation both as a focus of study and an approach to carrying out research and wanted to mitigate the risk of lapsing into objectifying discourses and contributing to processes of further marginalisation. However, the project that emerged was not just a consequence of deliberate decisions but also the unique relationships which formed amongst committed individuals who came together in response to a common cause.

At the first meeting, John informed me that *The Box* was at a juncture, having recently come to the end of a two-year Arts Council programme where eight artists had completed residences to enable participants to experience a variety of art forms including digital/visual art, theatre and music. As a consequence, many of the men had considerable history of engagement with the charity and were vocalising a desire to want to take a greater lead role in the organisation and activities. In this sense, rather than being *done to* in the space, they wanted to be *done with*, both in how they were expected to perform in the participative space and how their progression needs were realised. *The Box* had also recently been successful in securing a grant of £2,500 through the Royal Botanic Gardens Kew for a community horticultural project. By combining this with £5000 from the action-research work package of PARTISPACE, we were able to fund staffing and material costs for a substantial six-month arts-based project entitled *Lost and Found*.

From the outset, the men were clear that the wanted to use the arts to raise public awareness of experiences of homelessness in Manchester. Weekly workshops facilitated by John began with a number of brainstorming sessions of how to combine plants (a requirement of the funding of Kew gardens) and various experiences and feelings of the realities of being homeless. Ideas related to *guerrilla gardening* (Reynolds, 2009; McKay, 2011) in an attempt to occupy urban public space sparked the idea of creating planters, which could be erected as a temporary art installation in the city. There were also reoccurring themes of visibility and fears of being judged by the public whilst begging, evoking imagery of *freak shows* in Victorian Britain. The idea to create *viewing boxes* displaying aspects of homelessness thus sought to evoke dichotomies around being seen and unseen whilst inviting spectators to literally peer in, turn on the light and, through this act, put themselves in someone else's shoes (Figure 8.2). Furthermore, the flora and fauna contained in the planters enabled sensual engagement on a different level whilst aiming to occupy the urban space and attract spectators in a different way. For example, in one of the boxes the shame of washing in a public bathroom was depicted, whilst participants were made to feel like voyeurs as they peered in (Figure 8.3). Simultaneously, they could rub their fingers on the leaves of one of the plants, leaving a putrid, lingering smell.

Figure 8.2: One of the planters—entitled *A tramps bath*

Figure 8.3: Depiction of public bathroom inside viewing box of planter

Through discussion of common issues experienced by the men, five themes were decided upon which would be conveyed in each of the boxes. These included issues of privacy and personal hygiene, mental health, drug addiction, finding a place to sleep, and seeking support. The construction of the planters and boxes took place during weekly drop-in sessions at a local community garden centre for about three months. There was inconsistency in terms of which men attended mostly due to the nature of their lives but over the course of the project there were three men who took the lead and engaged most regularly. Once finished, the planters were temporarily installed in five locations in the city related to each theme. Despite attempts, we were unable to get official permission from the city council to do this and so the decision was taken to go *off the radar* and hope that no clash with the authorities resulted. Whilst the boxes were *in situ*, four walking tours were led by the men (Figure 8.4). Members of the public affiliated with *The Box* were invited to take part and through walking alongside, participants were invited to hear the men's stories and view the creative outputs of the project. Finally, a filmmaker, who attended the majority of the sessions and walking tours, made a film which charted the process of the project from beginning to end. Due to changes in group membership and restrictions on time, the men had limited involvement in how the film was edited but where possible their approval of the finished product was sought. The film was shown at a final exhibition, again to affiliated members including those working in similar social care and creative charities, third sector/government affiliated groups and academics.

Figure 8.4: Walking tour of planters led by the men from *The Box*

## 3. Ethnography and arts-based practices

Throughout the project, I adopted an ethnographic research approach; I recorded material through working with the filmmaker and kept a research diary. Rather than using interviews or observation, I fully participated in the activities and adopted a role akin to facilitator or volunteer. The men were used to student social workers coming in and out of the space often as part of work-based training placements but over time, they started to see how my role as a researcher was different. I was not there to try to encourage them to do x or y but instead I listened with attention and attunement (Weingarten, 2000) as I tried to oscillate between the position of insider and outsider. John was important in helping to establish my role in the group and as a skilled facilitator with experience of managing the presence of a researcher in the space; he was able to support trustful relationships to develop. As part of this process, the men tested emotional and physical boundaries and, at points, high levels of risk were present, which is part of the territory when working with people whose lives have been characterised by continual precarity. However, I showed I was willing to put the time in and accompany them; expose vulnerability (as they did to me) and also humour and frustration at the injustice of inequality. A willingness to get *stuck in* and engage in the making process of producing the installations whilst hearing stories of family relationships, love, trauma and violence as well as past, present and future hopes and regrets were all important features of building trust.

On a theoretical level, notions of accompaniment in both youth work and feminist approaches to ethnography have influenced my approach. In detached youth and community work, such forms of educational practice aim to remove barriers and engage people on their own terms (literally on the street), rather than expecting them to *come to us* to access support (Tiffany, 2012; 119; Crimmens, 2004). Similarly, in ethnography the importance of *hanging out* and *go-alongs* provide opportunities to observe participants in their everyday environments, enabling the researcher to gain an insider's perspective (Kusenbach, 2003). For example, I participated in outreach work and collected data as the men led us through the streets whilst practicing the walking tours. In feminist approaches to research, emphasis is placed upon reflexive approaches to fieldwork and analysis which aim to subvert power and answer the challenge of how to 'produce different knowledge and to produce knowledge differently' (Lather, 2002: 200). In this sense, I tried to create empathic spaces, which enabled knowledge to be co-created rather than exerting my power as the researcher. The use of participatory, arts-based practices facilitated such efforts because within the creative process there is space for collaboration and power to be exchanged. However, it is important not to romanticise ways that arts-based practices can transform the research process to magically conquer issues of power or issues of voice and representation. In the next section, I explore in more detail the data which was made visible and heard as a consequence to the use of arts-based practices but I also survey the limitations of the methodological approach. This reflexive approach seeks to recognise the unsatisfactory nature of the research encounter whilst engaging in broader debates about how we can open up opportunities for more democratic and inclusive participatory spaces.

## 4. The possibilities and limits of arts-based practices

Batsleer's (2011) earlier paper details how five aspects of arts-based practice were identified as opening up communicative possibilities for sex workers who were involved in a theatre production involving young male sex workers who accessed *The Box*. In this section, I discuss each of these in turn in relation to the *Lost and Found* project to explore how creativity enabled insights into the men's lives both in terms of their participation in *The Box* and within the research process itself.

Firstly, Batsleer (2011) recognises how through the use of the arts-based practices, symbolisation becomes immensely significant and enables participants to determine what is of importance. In this sense, they can control the agenda, unlike more traditional research approaches, which are often led and imposed by the researcher. In relation to the five installations made to raise awareness of homelessness for the *Lost and Found* project, the inside of the boxes were full of symbols. The viewing holes together with the light, invited participants to literally peer in and illuminate aspects of the men's lives through graphic descriptions on a miniature scale. The symbolic qualities of the creative processes supported participants to feel in control as they were able to give significance in literal and ambiguous ways. For example, in the film, Kyle, one of the participants, is shown picking the plants for the blue box, which depicted what it was like to wash in a public bathroom when homeless. He asked "what colour plant would express humiliation?"

Such reflections leads us to Batsleer's (2011) second aspect; arts-based practice requires expressions of feeling, something which many of the homeless men have been preconditioned and discouraged to do. The feelings evoked in the actual installations were opaque and invited the viewer to situate themselves whereas the stories told on the walking tours and the video conveyed, 'how voice can be more than merely rational; it's meaning contradictory, ambivalent, multiple, neither one thing or another' (Batsleer, 2011; 427). As shown later in the video, Luke can be encouraged by facilitators to practice the route of the walking tour, he can simultaneously resist, complain, and refuse to go because the weather is too hot, but then coin the catchy phrase which we used in some publicity materials for the project "hashtag lost and found get the message out there" and later emphatically assert "homelessness has taught me that you only get one shot at this life, you have got to get out there and make the most of it".

Such examples show the importance of provisionality and techniques that enable a helpful distance from ownership, which allow participants to try out different versions of themselves. As Batsleer (2011) identifies as her third aspect of arts-based practice, these processes are vital for creating opportunities for identity-making. For example, when taking a lead role, Luke often masqueraded as *Mr Supervisor*, trying to get others to do the work. However, playing the role of *the joker* disguised his transition from outsider to someone who started to have the confidence in his creative abilities and relationships with other group members. Such attempts are informed by youth and community arts pedagogies, which recognise that it is not beyond the bounds of imagination that occupying such positions within a safe environment may provide confidence to try out different versions of oneself in other parts of life.

As a fourth aspect, Batsleer (2011) notes that arts-based practice also involves a degree of risk-taking in committing and making the outputs public. In the case of the walking tours and the film exhibition, there was a sense that the men felt empowered from having the opportunity to talk about their personal experiences of homelessness, whilst raising awareness for others. In this sense, the power of their testimonies came from the authority of experience (Kandil, 2016), which in turn strengthened the human connection with audience members by making the unfamiliar, familiar. The power of the creative thus had the capacity to counter the aforementioned neo-liberal accounts of *haves* and *have nots* which fuel divisions and the demarcation of boundaries between those who are deemed to deserve help and those who do not. However, this is not to say that such practices are not without risk. Within the confines of *The Box*, the men's stories were judged as credible but as John, (creative director/facilitator) was keen to test out in preparation of the walking tours to selected members of the public, what if someone challenges you turns around and says "you should not be begging on the street, you should go out and get a job".

Although audience members responded positively, both facilitators and participants were acutely aware that some listeners may doubt their credibility, whilst the scale of challenge in the city meant that tensions were high. Such issues led to the decision that specific audience members would be invited who were likely to evoke encouraging and positive reactions. However, such decisions raise questions with regard to the potential reach and impact of the project. Such themes are explored in the following transcript extract from the discussion after the film showing.

*Audience member:* Who should see it? (in reference to the film), who should be in the audience?

*Kyle:* the lost generation of the homeless

*Luke:* anyone at all, urm ... I dunno

*Connor:* everyone should see, both sides of life, like the good side, and the bad side, there are many different sides otherwise people don't respect where people have come from, I think everyone should have an equal opportunity to see it.

*Audience member:* I was at a meeting the other week and we were told that there is no reason in Manchester for anyone to sleep rough and that is the council's version. So immediately, I think maybe you should tie the councillors down and get them to watch it.

*Audience member:* I don't understand why they say it is not needed ... I think there is a belief that support is not required.

Such difficulties in spheres of influence meant that at times the project also felt disempowering for the men. Within the confines of the space, we could support and accompany the men on their journey. As Batsleer (2011) recognises:

> There is a profound level of acceptance at work. Judgement is mediated through the arts practice and reframed as questioning and learning. This gives everyone freedom and a sense that something which usually remains hidden and unexplored can be spoken about.     (Batsleer, 2011; 428)

However, the sensitive and personal nature of many of the men's stories meant that when entering the public frame this exposed some vulnerability and feelings of alienation. Therefore, at times the process felt exploitative whilst there was a danger that by retelling their stories during the repeated walking tours or watching it back on film had re-traumatising effects and could be further stigmatising. Similar experiences have urged Kandil (2016) after performing in an applied theatre project to raise the following question:

> How many novice participants engage in this type of practice, whole-heartedly trusting the experience and end up feeling isolated and alone in facing the overwhelming feelings sometimes associated with telling and sharing their personal narratives? (Kandil, 2016; 212)

Interestingly, the men left out details in some of the stories they told during the course of the walking tours depending on who was in the audience. Although there was a sense of empowerment at the film exhibition, they were only nominally involved in the creation and editing of the film despite consenting to the footage being recorded. Such challenges have meant that we made the decision for the film not be made freely available on the internet and therefore it has had limited exposure.

Finally, Batsleer (2011; 428) identifies how creative-based work encourages playfulness, akin to being a child and imagine that 'another life is possible.' As Jason, another participant explained as he reflected on why his involvement in the *Lost and Found* project was significant to him:

> I could go to my mates but I dunno ... this is different. I feel like I should don a shield, (beating his chest), climb a mountain and take on three hundred people and scream *listen!* (takes a leap and throws his arms up) It's a chance to get a point across, a chance to be something else than the mundane. Like instead of just putting up with things and can have a chance to sway a different vote, change the balance a bit. To try and make a difference to something which often doesn't feel in your control.

Thus, the relational dimension of participation came to the fore; Jason felt empowered that he could affect broader change whilst in turn this has a positive impact on perceptions of his own self-efficacy.

## 5. Closing Discussion

More broadly, studies in young people's participation acknowledge that participation develops step-by-step alongside increasing self-efficacy and increasing consciousness of the public dimension of personal lives (Schwaenflugel,

2014; Walther, 2006). On a motivational level, these processes need to combine so that they can be understood as functional for one's own biography (Walther, 2006). At this point, it is important to acknowledge that as well as the agentic aspects of this project there were also incidences where involvement in *Lost and Found* also made the men aware of their own powerlessness. On a practical level, many of the men merely wanted to be in an economically viable position and obtain employment. However, structural and cultural processes of inequality further persist to make even the boldest attempts feel worthless and thus challenge a straightforward or expedient relationship between participation, the arts and self-efficacy. This raises questions about the extent to which arts and creative-based work can be positioned as a magic bullet which, unfortunately, is all-too-often the case in policy and funding arrangements in the social care and arts sector at present. This is not to say, as has been explored in this chapter, that arts-based practices cannot have considerable communicative possibilities giving opportunity for increased voice and representation of marginalised groups but, as well as their successes, it is important to acknowledge their limitations.

In conclusion, arts-based practices when used alongside an ethnographic approach greatly enhanced what was heard and made visible both in terms of understanding how styles of participation function in particular spaces but also participation in the research process. The limitations of the methodological approach show how it may be impossible to escape the power relations and pedagogic codes, which function in particular professional domains or contexts. However, there are moments of illumination where the struggle of symbolic capital is negotiated and this seems to be enabled in complex ways by arts-based practices. Such incidences of hope have potential in enabling us to think differently about how researchers, arts practitioners, researchers, youth and community workers, social workers and young people may work together to build more democratic, inclusive and participative practice.

## Acknowledgements

I am eternally grateful to the staff and men at *The Box* for supporting this research project. In accordance with ethics procedures, I have not been able to name them so pseudonyms have been used. I continue to grapple with these ethical complexities and try to find other ways to acknowledge their contribution.

# References

Arnot, M. and Reay, D., (2007) A sociology of pedagogic voice, power, inequality and pupil consultation, *Discourse: Studies in the Cultural Politics of Education,* 28(3):311-25.

Batsleer, J., (2011) Voices from an edge: Unsettling the practices of youth voice and participation: arts-based practice in The Blue Room, Manchester, *Pedagogy, Culture and Society,* 19(3):419-434.

Crimmens, D., (2004) *Reaching socially excluded young people: A national study of street-based youth work,* Leicester: Joseph Rowntree Foundation National Youth Agency.

Enria, L., (2016) Co-producing knowledge through participatory theatre: Reflections on ethnography, empathy and power, *Qualitative Research,* 16(3):319-329.

Geertz, C.,(1973) *The interpretation of cultures,* New York: Basic Books.

Holland, S., Renold, E., Ross, N. J. and Hillman, A., (2010) Power agency and participatory agendas: A critical exploration of young people's engagement in participative qualitative research, *Childhood,* 17(3):360-337.

Lather, P., (2002) Postbook: Working the ruins of feminist ethnography, *Signs: A Journal of Women in Culture and Society,* 27(1):199-227.

McKay, G., (2011) *Radical gardening: Politics, idealism and rebellion in the garden,* London: Frances Lincoln.

Newton, K., (2001) Trust, social capital, civil society, and democracy, *International Political Science Review,* 22(2):201-14.

Percy-Smith, B. and Thomas, N. (eds.), (2010) *A handbook of children and young people's participation. Perspectives from theory and practice,* London: Routledge.

Polkinghorne, D. E., (1996) Transformative narratives: From victimic to agentic life plots, *American Journal of Occupational Therapy,* 50(4):299-305.

Reynolds, R., (2008) *On guerrilla gardening: A handbook for gardening without permission,* London: Bloomsbury.

Sinha, S. and Back, L., (2014) Making methods sociable: Dialogue, ethics and authorship in qualitative research. *Qualitative Research,* 14(4):473-487

Schwanenfluegel, L., (2014) *Partizipationsbiographien Jugendlicher: Zur Bedeutung von Partizipation im Kontext sozialer Ungleichheit [Participation biographies of young people: Relevance of participation in the context of social inequality],* Wiesbaden: VS Springer

Thomson, P. (ed.), (2008) *Doing visual research with children and young people,* London:Routledge.

Walther, A., (2006) Regimes of youth transitions, *Young,* 14(2):119-139.

Weingarten, K., (2000) Witnessing, wonder and hope, *Family Process,* 39(4):389-402.

Wrigley, T., Thomson, P. and Lingard, B. (eds.), (2012) *Changing schools: Alternative ways to make a world of difference,* London: Routledge.

Yeung, P., (2016) Homelessness in England rises 54% since 2010' *The Independent.* Accessed on 3rd January 2018. http://www.independent.co.uk/news/uk/home-news/homelessness-housing-households-shelter-london-england-a7111501.html

# Chapter 9

## The reinvention of a peripheral neighbourhood in Lisbon: Reflections on urban art, ethnography and public policy

*Otávio Raposo[1]*

### 1. Introduction

Quinta do Mocho, located in the district of Loures, has become known in the media as one of the major *problematic neighbourhoods* in the Lisbon metropolitan area, a label based on the supposed relationship between its young residents and crime. But the reason that is currently putting Quinta do Mocho in the news is art, since the area has been transformed into one of the most important urban art hotspots in Portugal, with more than seventy large-scale works (graffiti, paintings, sculptures) decorating the social housing buildings that are home to roughly 3,000 people.

Originally subversive, illegal and non-commercial (Campos, 2010; Ferro, 2016), graffiti is undergoing the effects of *artification* (Shapiro and Heinich, 2013). Its reconfiguration by several agents—local authorities, the media, academia, urbanists, cultural entrepreneurs—have changed its *marginal* status to legitimise it in the art world. It is against this backdrop that the once-maligned graffiti is transformed into urban art, becoming immersed in commercial processes that serve the goals of planning, promoting and resolving a city's social issues. This is the case of the Quinta do Mocho public art gallery (*Galeria de Arte Pública*—GAP), a project organised by Loures Municipal Council (LMC) which began in 2014, that is changing the way the neighbourhood is seen by the outside world and involves the participation of some young residents. They are the ones leading the guided tours, on which they present a perspective different from the traditional stereotypes. While artistic expressions are excellent ways to overcome segregation and stigmatisation processes among subaltern groups, it is important to debate their limits and the political exploitation of art when approaching social issues. In this situation, ethnography is an important ally for

1. Otávio Raposo is an invited Assistant Professor at the Anthropology Department of University Institute of Lisbon (ISCTE-IUL) and postdoctoral researcher at the Centre for Research and Studies in Sociology (CIES-IUL). This chapter is funded by FCT—Fundação para a Ciência e a Tecnologia under the project «UID/SOC/03126/2013» and was translated from Portuguese by Tom Williams.

the researcher, allowing him or her to look at the situation *from within* (Burgess, 1997), encouraging *dense descriptions* of what is at stake beneath the surface (Geertz, 2008).

## 2. Ethnography at the Quinta do Mocho public art gallery

Transformed into one of the largest open-air urban art galleries in Europe, Quinta do Mocho has attracted thousands of tourists from Portugal and abroad since 2015 (according to LMC, roughly 1500 people visited the neighbourhood in 2016 as part of the guided tours organised by GAP, a number that rose to more than 3000 in 2017). This would have been unthinkable a few years ago, when the area was characterised as one of transgression and *anomie*. This process of change offers enormous wealth if approached using ethnography based on its central figures, the community guides. It is largely thanks to them that the neighbourhood has ultimately been reclassified by politicians and the media. But there was another reason that led me to visit Quinta do Mocho.

My initial research objective was to focus on Spot, a social project supported by the Choices Program (*Programa Escolhas*, or PE) operating in the area. It was at that project that I met Kedy, in 2015, one of the most active community guides, whose collaboration with LMC was in its early stages. Faced with the metamorphosis that the neighbourhood was going through and its excellent position for reflecting on that process, I changed the focus of the research, and began to accompany the guides on the tours they ran in the everyday spaces which they frequented.

The first trips in the field were made in 2015, but it was only in February 2016 that I began to visit Quinta do Mocho regularly for the ethnographic immersion that required forty-eight field trips to January 2018. Ethnography was an excellent instrument for understanding, beyond the institutional outlook, the implementation of that public policy from below, in the places where the urban art actions and the residents' experiences occurred (Trouillot, 2011). To become familiar with the urban art project, at the beginning of the research I chose to explore the guided tours ethnographically. These were excellent moments for understanding the representations and feelings of *urbanness* given to the neighbourhood and those who live there.

The guided tours enabled me to have access to a very rich situational context where I got to see not only the symbolic interpretation of the artworks made by the guides but also the public image of Quinta do Mocho which it was hoped would be transmitted based on the regeneration process launched by GAP.

The fact that the tours happen every month on set days and times, generally Saturday mornings, was also helpful because I was able to find the guides without making arrangements with them beforehand. I made an effort to make a careful participant observation of those tours, when I recorded audio, took photographs and made notes in the field, experiences that would be further explored in the following days based on the field diary. The conversations with guides during and, most of all, after the tours were valuable. These informal meetings enabled controversial topics to be discussed and elicited critiques of GAP itself. From that immersion in the field, two visions of the urban art project stood out: one *official*, performed in presentations about the area's artworks, and the other *informal*, based on questions from tourists or in the relaxed setting of a conversation. In fact, I sought a view *from close-up and within* (Magnani, 2002) of the effects of GAP with community guides and residents, which forced me to learn about their experiences and worldviews. This does not mean uncritically reproducing the *native* viewpoint but transforming that experience of otherness into new knowledge (Magnani, 2009). This opinion is shared by Michel Agier (2011), for whom the rationales of *making the city*, observed ethnographically based on citizens' concrete experiences and their movements through the metropolis, express his proposed anthropology of the city.

After participating in some tours, I focused on the relationship between the community guides and other young people in other dense settings full of sociability and symbolic value: street parties, urban art events and informal meetings in the street or at neighbourhood cafés. While the Spot Association was an excellent meeting point, deepening friendship relationships allowed me to seek people out directly at their homes, where we discussed topics that went beyond GAP: life in the neighbourhood, migratory journeys, music and art, racism, and similar topics. All the interviews took place at Quinta do Mocho, some of them at the young people's homes and others at quiet places in the area. The in-depth, semi-structured interviews with the two main community guides were important for getting to know their biographical journeys, the complexities of the neighbourhood and GAP, as well as the disputes regarding this public policy. In addition, I interviewed another ten people including community leaders and workers at non-governmental organisations (NGOs), artists and/ or Quinta do Mocho residents, along with LMC representatives.

The fact that my young interlocutors live in a municipal neighbourhood belonging to LMC, in a situation of certain vulnerability compared to the public authority, raised ethical questions for me about how I would describe my observations without harming them. In ethnography, the researcher should become involved with the people he/she studies intimately and respectfully, taking the utmost care not to expose them to compromising situations. I therefore did not use information that could cause problems for the people involved, guaranteeing the right to anonymity whenever necessary. As in the guides' case this was not possible—even if I used fake names, they would always be recognisable—I increased those ethical precautions, sharing (and discussing) the text with them before submitting it for publication.

One of the ethnographic discoveries of that research was a tense episode involving residents and LMC when Vhils, a renowned Portuguese artist, was going to paint the face of a young man from the neighbourhood called DJ Nervoso. Although I did not witness the scene, I collected statements from the people involved so I could perform a situation analysis of the conflict. The importance of incorporating that analysis in the article is due to the fact that the conflict was an extraordinarily paradigmatic situation illustrating the antagonism and contradictions surround the public policy and it also serves to understand some of its outcomes after the strong position taken by the residents in that episode. Following the teachings of J. Clyde Mitchell (2009), situation analysis is an effective methodological instrument for understanding a broader context, forming an excellent *window of analysis* for understanding interactions between agents that are positioned unequally in a certain territory.

## 3. Going into Quinta do Mocho

On the last Saturday of each month, LMC organises a guided tour of the pieces at Quinta do Mocho open to all those interested in urban art. With the aim of taking part in one of those tours, I went to the Sacavém House of Culture (*Casa da Cultura de Sacavém*), the meeting point, on a Saturday morning. Surprised by the large number of people, around seventy people, I caught sight of the *cicerones* (guides) Kedy, aged thirty, and Kally, aged thirty-seven, two of the project's community guides. They were talking with council workers who were directing visitors to the building's entrance. Before the tour, there would be a short speech by the councillor Maria Eugénia Coelho. With the two guides by her side, the councilor reminded the audience of the time when Quinta do Mocho was a collection of unfinished tower blocks surrounded by a shanty town due to the bankruptcy of construction firm J. Pimenta. They were occupied, from the 1980s onward, by immigrants from Portuguese-speaking African countries (known as PALOPs, or *Países de Língua Oficial Portuguesa*, in Portuguese), particularly

Angola, São Tomé and Príncipe, Guinea-Bissau, and Cape Verde. The councilor highlighted the poor living conditions of that time:

The living conditions were terrible. Every last space was turned into a house and around 3,000 people lived there in very poor conditions. There was an urgent need to resolve the problem. With the Special Rehousing Program, Loures Municipal Council built this neighbourhood to rehouse those people. And in 2000-2001, people settled there. [Maria Eugénia Coelho. Field diary—30 April 2016]

Built on an area close to the former occupied towers, today's Quinta do Mocho is formed of ninety-one buildings with around 800 apartments. In her address, the councilor highlighted the fact that Quinta do Mocho's residents were *good people* and *hard-working*, underlining the role played by women (and mothers) in supporting families during the economic crisis. The rise in unemployment from 2009 onward heavily affected the civil construction sector, in which a substantial part of male residents worked. After reporting the neglect of Quinta do Mocho during the previous legislature, the councilor contextualised the intervention of the current LMC, with the emergence of GAP in the area. Maria Eugénia said, regarding the importance of this public policy:

This project alone is very worthwhile because there are more than fifty-one pieces, but we really want to underline the change that the neighbourhood has seen in attitude, in its very physical structures, in the cleanliness that the residents themselves also demand and take part in. In control, in self-control, when young children do something silly, people don't let them. The pride that we need was actually returned to the neighbourhood.

[Maria Eugénia Coelho. Field diary—30 April 2016]

Kally then greeted the audience, speaking with a northern accent about his past as a writer in Porto. Kedy also welcomed the visitors, underscoring *safety tips* to follow in the neighbourhood. He was joking about the stereotypes surrounding Quinta do Mocho, since he was not talking about *bad things* but instead the care to take regarding traffic in the area's streets. A resident of Quinta do Mocho for sixteen years, Kedy talked in a mysterious tone:

We also have a few little surprises here that we decided to bring with us today to help make the project sustainable. This is the first day. We've made some merchandise to help the young people who do the guided tours and also find future solutions for the project, and we'll be showing them to you later.

[Kedy. Field diary—30 April 2016]

### 4. 'Everything's changed now, we're not a ghetto anymore': Ethnography of the guided tours

Led by Kedy and Kally, we entered Quinta do Mocho on *avenida* Amílcar Cabral (avenue), where we saw the image of the African leader covering one of the buildings. Kedy pointed out the importance of this historical figure for all Africans, a reason for pride in a neighbourhood where almost all the residents have their origins in that continent. When explaining the impact that the murals had for the people who live there, Kedy reiterated the idea of Quinta do Mocho as a *problematic neighbourhood* marked not only by stigma but by unemployment, poverty and behavioural problems: crime, violence and low self-esteem. Following this example, the GAP project came to 'change the neighbourhood's situation', involving a 'transformation and regeneration process'.

Figure 9.1: Amílcar Cabral (Photograph by Otávio Raposo)

One of the emblematic images of Quinta do Mocho can be found in the same street: a black woman taking off a white mask. Created by the artist Nomen, Kally connected this allegory to the stigma the area held and which residents experienced on a daily basis, with a negative effect when job hunting.

> This graffiti really represents that: it is the mask. Here in the neighbourhood, we are what we are, and when we would leave the neighbourhood to look for work, we had to say we were from somewhere else. (...) Out there, we had to say we were from Sacavém, Bobadela or somewhere else. That was the only way we could move on to the next stage in the recruitment process, that was the only way we could get a job, because we could never say we were from here.                                    [Kally. Audio recording—30 April 2016]

Figure 9.2: The mask (Photograph by Otávio Raposo)

When we go into the square, we see murals of female figures, an homage to the area's women. One of them is *black Athena*, an adaptation of the Greek goddess of wisdom and warfare. Holding a spear with a snake wrapped around it, the figure is accompanied by a reddish owl, attributes relating to Athena. The artist behind the design, a Catalan named Alexis, explained to me months later that his goal was to give the neighbourhood a feminine touch without resorting to clichés:

(...) I wanted to draw or represent an idea of ... an ideal of a woman that was not an aesthetic ideal of the 21st century, you know? Where she has to have plastic tits, she has to dress a certain way, but rather an icon of a universal woman, in this case the goddess Athena, who for the Greeks was the best-known goddess and represents... could represent beauty or wisdom or warfare or other things...you know?

[Alexis. Interview at Quinta do Mocho—22 June 2016]

Beside this image, the painting of a man playing the piano symbolises the musical activities present in the neighbourhood. This is because Quinta do Mocho *breathes music*, as Kedy (himself a rapper) explains to us, and there are many singers, DJs, producers and dancers.

On the way to the top of the neighbourhood we went past a piece by Smile, whose design, of a giraffe on the body of a child, is impressive in its size and realism. One of the most vigilant creatures in the animal kingdom, the giraffe has the largest heart of all terrestrial animals. These two characteristics inspired Smile, who observed the *great heart* of Quinta do Mocho's residents, and their sense of caution upon the arrival of outsiders. We all laugh at Kally's explanation, and he mentions the fact that guides always accompany artists when they do their work, and find out the reasons behind each piece. When asked how the themes were chosen, Kally said that artists were given complete freedom to choose as they wished. The same visitor who asked the previous question then asked about how residents participated in the process, and she was given the following reply:

Almost all the artists who come here stay with us. They walk around with us for a couple of days and put something in their painting about that experience. Almost all the artists are inspired to paint by the community.

[Kally. Field diary—30 April 2016]

I would later find out that themes were chosen by the artists often before coming to the neighbourhood. They would send a mock-up of the design to LMC so it could be approved (and selected) among other proposals, and the dates of each intervention would be established.

In front of one piece by Vhils—one of the most renowned Portuguese artists—Kedy highlighted that the neighbourhood was home to noteworthy producers and DJs of a new electronic rhythm called *batida* (a kind of electronic *kuduro*[2] with a beat provided by music production software in a fusion of

2. type of music and dance originally developed in Angola and Portugal in the 1980s.

different styles: from *funaná*[3] to Afro House, from electro music to Afrobeat), whose influence in Lisbon had not gone unnoticed by national and international media. This was the dynamic that inspired Vhils to paint the face of the DJ Nervoso, a decision that did not please a substantial number of the area's young people.

> Vhils found out on the internet that there were some young people working with electronic music who are finding success abroad in international magazines such as Rolling Stone, Times and others. Based on the information he gathered about those people, he discovered that DJ Nervoso, a young man who has lived in the neighbourhood for many years, was widely admired because he was the one who grew the musical style that is so successful today. And he did the piece based on that. At first, it caused some commotion because people here didn't think that anyone had the right to have their face on a wall. [Kedy. Audio recording—30 April 2016]

The Bob Marley picture stands out at the top of the neighbourhood. Created by Odeith, the mural almost resulted in *chaos*, in the words of one guide, discussing the intimidating action taken by the police when they saw a group of young people watching it be painted.

With the sun directly above our heads, we had a quick break at Elsa, a restaurant enjoyed for its *cachupa*[4] and other delicacies. This was one of the rare moments of interaction between residents and tourists, whose presence was ignored by the few residents walking around the area at that time. While we quenched our thirst, one of the guides spoke about the transformations in the neighbourhood that were a result of the murals:

> Two or three years ago, you wouldn't come here. Not because you'd be mugged, but because the media told you not to. Everything's changed now, we're not a ghetto any more. [Kally. Field diary—30 April 2016]

---

It is characterised as uptempo, energetic, and danceable. Kuduro began in Luanda, Angola in the late 1980s. Producers sampled traditional carnival music like *soca* and *zouk* from the Caribbean, *semba* from Angola, Techno and Accordion playing from Europe and laid this around a fast 4/4 beat, Wikipedia.

3. a music and dance genre from Cape Verde. Funaná is an accordion-based music. It is perhaps the most upbeat form of Cape Verdean music.

4. Cachupa is a famous dish from the Cape Verde islands, West Africa. This slow cooked stew of corn (hominy), beans, cassava, sweet potato, fish or meat (sausage, beef, goat or chicken) is often referred to as the country's national dish.

We left the café and saw *Heron* by Bordalo II, an installation created using scrap found at the junkyard, summarised by Kally as follows: "Luxury can be made from trash". We were crossing one of the neighbourhood's squares when Kedy pointed out the Catholic church and mosque operating in the same building: "This is the faith area; the faith and culture area". We were at the heart of the neighbourhood, where a stage set up by the borough council overlooked the many cultural and religious activities that took place there. While the stigmatisation of Quinta do Mocho residents was been commonplace, the lack of visibility of their cultural practices that offer them a dignified identity appears to be the other side of the same coin. To work against that trend, Kedy discussed some of the *neighbourhood talents*, from people with higher education to musicians and football players, and then went on to show us the building where the former Sporting player Carlos Mané grew up.

We were shown another piece by Vhils, this time made using a collage of overlapping newspapers and photographs. A large eye dominates the panel, which includes unfinished buildings in an allusion to the former Quinta do Mocho. One of the last pieces discussed during the tour was of a woman, her face covered by a scarf, accompanied by paintbrushes, pencils, pens and spray cans on her back. Made by the artist *Pinta com que há* (Paint with what there is), it represents the transgressive and clandestine nature of the graffiti world, a situation that Kally links to the criminalisation of writers as well as Quinta do Mocho residents:

> Here in the neighbourhood, we also had to hide ourselves, just like the writers had to use tags so they wouldn't be recognised.
>
> [Kally. Field diary—30 April 2016]

We were on our way back to the House of Culture at the end of the tour when a man asked one of the guides if they received any payment from LMC. The man seemed shocked to find out that they were not paid for the tours they led: "but you should be paid for that work". Later on in the conversation, Kedy said:

> We're the ones who drive the tours. The knowledge and contributions of young people in the neighbourhood are fundamental. The tours began after the art had been here for a year. (...) People see opportunities. It's magic here.
>
> [Kedy. Field diary—30 April 2016]

Without asking for any kind of contribution from visitors, the guides sold magnets and badges with images of the artworks in the neighbourhood for two euros. Once they said goodbye to the visitors, they added up and split the money they had made, putting part of it aside to pay to make future products.

## 5. Disputes about the Vhils piece: When residents want to have an active voice

When talking with Quinta do Mocho residents, we can quickly see that most approved of the murals because they contribute to a positive image of the area. However, residents' participation in GAP is limited. They are not the ones who choose the themes painted on the walls of the buildings where they live, nor were there residents painting or learning to do graffiti at the organised events. The theme is usually chosen by the artists before they have been to the neighbourhood, a process which is entirely mediated by LMC. Many residents find out their buildings are going to be painted on the day itself by the noise of the cranes used by the artists. Denied their right to speak, residents' participation in creating the images and symbolism of each piece is therefore quite limited and dependent on the artist's sensitivity in incorporating them in the creative process. Several residents questioned this reasoning when Vhils was about to draw the face of DJ Nervoso on the façade of one of the buildings in June 2015. Vhils' initial idea was to paint DJ Marfox, slated by the North American magazine *Rolling Stone* as one of the 'ten new artists you need to know in 2014'. This fame did not go unnoticed by Vhils, who wanted to pay homage to Quinta do Mocho with an image of the renowned resident. Marfox did not grow up in the neighbourhood and only lived there recently. So he did not think it was fair to have his image transposed to the wall, suggesting instead DJ Nervoso who, as well as growing up in Quinta do Mocho, was one of the forefathers of the music style they championed.

Figure 9.3: DJ Nervoso (Photograph by Otávio Raposo)

Together with staff from LMC and DJs from the neighbourhood, Vhils was planning the painting of Nervoso on the wall to start work when some young people came up to him to ask about what would happen. Until then, no one in the neighbourhood had been *distinguished* with their face on the wall, given the GAP principle of allowing only abstract, fictional or historical figures to be shown. The image of Nervoso therefore opened a precedent. As soon as they were told that Nervoso's face would be painted, the young people were outraged, leading to a heated discussion that attracted other residents. They did not think it was fair that the decision had been made without discussing it with residents beforehand: some said that Nervoso was not an uncontentious enough person to have his face shown on the wall, others criticised the sudden *change in the rules*, since the local authority had guaranteed them that they would never use the image of a neighbourhood resident.

Hélder was one of the youngsters who were against the picture of Nervoso from the very beginning, and he believed that the episode "is an example not only of a lack of voice but of their [the local authority's] unwillingness to listen to us". This confrontation was very clear in his memory:

There were loads of people there, loads of people. Firmino, a guy who's in prison now, asked: "What's going on here?", "We're going to paint Nervoso's face". That caused trouble. "You guys are going to paint Nervoso's face with whose permission?", "Who did you ask? You never asked anyone about anything. We thought that it would be paintings of abstract things, an idea comes into your head and you do it, not painting the faces of people from the area. Because if the idea is to paint the faces of local people, there are people who are more important to us than Nervoso."

[Hélder. Interview at Quinta do Mocho—15 August 2017]

According to Hélder, the people involved did not have any kind of personal issue with Nervoso, some even remembered the parties he ran in the area (DJ Nervoso was one of those involved in the *kaduro* parties held inside the area's empty shops between 2003 and 2007, giving rise to a booming music scene that decisively contributed to the creation of the *batida* style). It was the local authority's lack of sensitivity in failing to hear the residents that produced the revolt, the last straw in a wider build-up of dissatisfaction. The deaths of two local young people, one of whom lived in the building where the mural was to be painted, also stoked tensions.

Faced with a threat to destroy the mural or even burn down the building if the project went ahead, Vhils and the LMC staff members suspended the initiative. They decided to change the original location for the work, shifting Nervoso's image from one of the neighbourhood's busiest streets to one of the edges. Vhils' ability to understand the reasons behind the rebellion have been praised by Roberto, aged twenty-seven, another young man from Quinta do Mocho:

It was really something! Because imagine having more than a hundred people saying: "We don't want you to paint! Get out of here!" That's not normal. It was hard for them to hear what they heard, but Vhils was able to understand them. (...) Everyone there, nobody was spared, everyone was insulted at the time. So Vhils ... That's when you see who's a big person and who's a small person. [Roberto. Interview at Quinta do Mocho—9 September 2016]

With the *wounds* of that episode still open, Vhils suggested a design for the *contentious* wall that told the stories of the neighbourhood through photographs of the residents themselves. The new collaborative project was supported by Kedy, who collected the donated photographs. With the old unfinished buildings at the top, the panel contains a large eye with photographs of the residents around it, an initiative that people welcomed.

Figure 9.4: The eye (Photograph by Otávio Raposo)

The limited dialogue the local authority had with Quinta do Mocho residents about the dynamics of GAP is a fundamental part of understanding that revolt. It expressed the dissatisfaction of people who live in a precarious urban setting, marked by silencing and imposition, a situation common to many of those who live in social housing. The position of strength demonstrated by residents in the Vhils episode called attention to their right not only to negotiate and make suggestions but also to question the real benefits that they would get from the urban art project, when there was a series of unresolved grievances which were seen as more urgent: leaks in apartments, mosquito infestations, run-down leisure areas, lack of cleanliness, missing doors at building entrances, no bus running through the neighbourhood, etc. This issue was described by Roberto:

> That commotion needed to happen for the people who are always in the neighbourhood, the unemployed, to claim their rights. And they were right to do so (...). It's nice for the Council people to appear in Público [newspaper], but it makes no difference for the people who live in the neighbourhood. People want to have a better life (...). Now there's a bus, there's better access, they clean the area every week. I don't know if you noticed, but there are always people cleaning. They did some draining, but there's still a lot of water underneath the buildings, they have to do more.
>
> [Roberto. Interview at Quinta do Mocho—9 September 2016 ]

Forced to review some of its normal procedures, LMC enhanced the channels for Quinta do Mocho residents to participate with the public authority by recruiting young people from the neighbourhood to be community guides. The involvement of *native* operators to promote GAP and resolve any possible problems became essential to the project's effectiveness, as well as providing the Council with excellent mediators with the population.

Community assemblies in Quinta do Mocho also provided a new boost. Residents could use the assemblies to make requests and demand structural improvements that went beyond the artworks. As Kedy explained: "The Council having to hold community assemblies was the graffiti's greatest victory". This new joining of forces meant LMC had to meet some of the residents' historical demands. Now there are bus routes running through the neighbourhood, doors at building entrances, ramps for disabled people were installed and cleaning services now run more regularly. Several problems persist, however, many of which are the result of the buildings' lack of maintenance, which is made worse by the poor construction quality. One of the worst is currently the large number of mosquitoes in the neighbourhood, a result of water leakages in the buildings' basements, which have become great breeding grounds.

## 6. The leaders of regenerating a neighbourhood

Turned into an *urban art hotspot*, with the vast production of large-scale pieces that include the work of the renowned Portuguese urban artists Odeith, Bordalo II, Nomen and Vhils, Quinta do Mocho's external image has changed, partially challenging the stereotype of urban violence associated with it. The change in representations in the media can be seen in the following newspaper and magazine headlines: Urban Art to recover Quinta do Mocho's image [*Arte Urbana para recuperar imagem da Quinta do Mocho*] (DN, 2014); A problematic area transformed into a Public Art Gallery [*Um bairro problemático transformado em Galeria de Arte Pública*] (TSF, 2015); The area no-one wants to go into now has 'more visitors than museums' [*O bairro onde ninguém quer entrar já 'recebe mais visitas que os museus'*] (Borges, 2016).

This recognition by the media, however, was highly indebted to the labour of community guides, responsible for enhancing the public visibility of the neighbourhood and attracting visitors. The guides' interpretation of the urban art collection that shapes the area is at the foundation of a process of cultural translation that makes use of street art to deal with the social context of Quinta do Mocho, also addressing the alleged *regeneration* the neighbourhood is undergoing. As one of the guides states about GAP:

> It's transformative, it's important, it's inspiring. This neighbourhood needed something like that in order to change, it was an opportunity (...). Because there were lots of people who covered themselves with masks, they were embarrassed to go to school and say they were from Quinta do Mocho, they were embarrassed to look for a job since they knew they wouldn't be able to get one because they were from Quinta do Mocho. That stigma was very present. (...) And deep down the negative association is transforming into a positive one.     [Kedy. Interview at Quinta do Mocho—18 April 2016]

The participation of young people from Quinta do Mocho was fundamental to enabling the guided tours and overcoming people's initial misgivings about the project. The tours were carried out intermittently during a first stage and then became regular after the conflicts involving Vhils. It was at that time that the urban art project shifted from *O bairro i o mundo* (The neighborhood is the world) to become GAP, when the number of artworks grew exponentially and murals became the favoured way of regenerating the neighbourhood.

The inclusion of community guides was a key element in reconnecting the urban art project drawn up by LMC by making them the main promoters of the public policy. After a first period to approach and win over young people, their involvement in GAP was founded on taking responsibility in the supposed regeneration process the neighbourhood was undergoing. Encouraged to *do their bit*, Kedy and Kally were invited to be community guides, a task that was presented as a civic practice and a chance to transform the neighbourhood. However, it also involved providing services to the local authority free of charge, which was euphemistically called *volunteer work*.

LMC's action follow the recommendations from international organisations like the UN or UNESCO (Souza, 2008), in which *youth engagement* is one of the foundations of their integration policies. The principle of this is to transform young people into *protagonists* in the search for solutions to problems faced in their areas. However, that participation model may cause what Regina Souza believes to be a 'cancellation of the policy' (2008: 12), in that it offers few chances for autonomous and emancipatory discourse. Converted into *young people-solutions* (Souza, 2008; Tommasi, 2013), their dreams, energies and even rebellions are trapped by management devices (whether public or private) that act on populations in 'social vulnerability' situations, some playing the role of *mediator* and *leader* in cultural projects understood as *community* projects. In fact, the Mocho guides were introduced not just as intermediaries of the local authority but as examples to be followed by other young people and they would embody the successful regeneration process in the neighbourhood.

That Kedy was asked to be a community guide is not surprising. He is identified by residents as a community leader and an artist in the hip-hop scene, promoting collective actions through art and association-based activities. Born on the island of São Tomé and Príncipe, Kedy came to Portugal at the age of sixteen, moving to Quinta do Mocho with his family in 2002 at a time when the rehousing process was still ongoing. The strangeness of leaving a calm country to live in a large metropolis marked the first stages of his adaptation, when he experienced the adversities of residential segregation first hand.

> When I got here, the first thing I noticed was: "Oh, I've left one island to come to another one". Unfortunately, Quinta do Mocho was an island, there was nothing around it, there was no health center, supermarket, buses didn't come in here, it was really sad. There started to be problems with juvenile delinquency, family breakdown and there were a lot of conflicts. And we had never had problems like that, when we got here we were a bit shocked.
>
> [Kedy. Interview at Quinta do Mocho—20 February 2016]

Joining the *Império Suburbano* [Suburban Empire] rap collective enhanced Kedy's mediation qualities, encouraging him to go beyond the boundaries of Quinta do Mocho and multiply his friendship networks. As time went by, he would become an example for the young people in Quinta do Mocho, helping set up *Associação Jovens Estrelas do Bairro* [the Young Stars of the Neighbourhood Association]. Kedy recently finished a degree in Chemical Engineering at university, and is looking for a job in this field.

Kally's passion for the world of graffiti was crucial to his becoming a community guide. A Quinta do Mocho resident between 2001 and 2004 and again since 2012, Kally was raised by his grandmother in Porto, where he learned the secrets of graffiti when it was still considered a marginal art form. Born in Angola, his mother brought him to Portugal to escape the civil war when he was four years old. He did not complete his secondary education and has more than ten years' experience working in call centers. This has sharpened his skills as a performer and a promoter. The charisma he transmits to tourists on tours reveals the satisfaction he gets from promoting Quinta do Mocho, a way of fighting the stigma of what is now his home:

> I've always found it easy and enjoyed dealing with the public, but I'm not a salesman, I'm a promoter. And promoting my neighbourhood brings me a lot of satisfaction. It really satisfies me to change people's awareness, it really satisfies me to start a tour and see that the people at the back are a bit afraid, and when we get to the middle of the tour and those people who were further back are now right at the front. Seeing people's faces change when they come in here a bit suspicious and get to the middle or end of the tour and say that it was one of the best things they'd seen: not just the neighbourhood but the way we presented it. [Kally. Interview at Quinta do Mocho—11 April 2017]

Doing something they like for the neighbourhood's benefit was an initial encouragement for Kedy and Kally to agree to be volunteer guides. However, the economic pressure of unemployment and the growing number of guided tours increased the contradictions of not receiving any financial support from the local authority. The situation was even more controversial in Kally's case, since he has a son in his care.

Along with the rhetoric of volunteer work as a way to encourage the *regeneration of the neighbourhood*, LMC also required the guided tours to be free to the tourists, since GAP is a social project run by the local authority. The solution for the guides' growing dissatisfaction was to encourage them to become entrepreneurs. Attracted by that discourse, Kedy and Kally created merchandising products to be sold to tourists, a way of getting income and making the project sustainable. However, the amounts earned from selling the products were not enough to even provide basic sustenance.

Despite all the difficulties, Kedy and Kally still hope to transform the guided tours into a viable employment alternative. This dream is fed by both the pleasure of helping change the neighbourhood's image and by the *feeling of citizenship* (Arantes, 2000: 47) arising from creative work that provides them with some recognition. Disappointed with the bureaucracy and unwillingness of the local authority to change the precarious state in which they found themselves, they began to organise guided tours independently from LMC, charging tourists a small amount. This does not mean they will not carry on cooperating with the local authority, a relationship that is not always harmonious, depending on the way the interests surrounding GAP are disputed.

## 7. Final remarks

The beneficial effects of GAP in fighting the stigmatisation of Quinta do Mocho must be recognised, since the neighbourhood has started to be given as an example in the news as a reference point for urban art in Portugal and is no longer exclusively connected to themes of violence. Symbolically converted into an area of art and culture, Quinta do Mocho has been integrated into the country's tourism routes and is visits by people from outside the neighbourhood has became commonplace. The observations made using the ethnography methods revealed, however, that this public policy attempt to produce new feelings of *urbanness* in the area has not been free from contradictions. The fact that the residents have no decision-making power over the paths to be followed by the urban art project and other policies that deal with their area is an example of how they are not subjects to be heard, but objects embodied in the discourse. By relegating the residents' priorities to second place, GAP restates their subaltern state, denying them the condition of *builders of the city* (Holston, 2013: 30). With the revolt surrounding Vhils' painting, the residents demonstrated their dissatisfaction with that subaltern status and took a strong position in an attempt to influence the urban art project in their territory and exercise their *right to the city* (Lefebvre, 1999). Furthermore, the tours of the neighbourhood led by community guides reveal unforeseen uses of the street, claiming *ways of doing* (de Certeau, 1980) that are more critical, autonomous and sustainable. Both cases highlight the importance of incorporating the sensitivity of those who live in the neighbourhood and the need for more democratic public policies. From that viewpoint, the public space of Quinta do Mocho cannot be merely a multicultural setting for tourists to visit, nor should the murals decorate precariousness for residents. As the stage for intense socialisations, the neighbourhood's streets are privileged areas of memory and affection among residents, where identities and feelings of belonging are built that support their understanding of the world. Incorporating that *experienced* perspective is fundamental for us to gain a more complex view of the public policies in action, a knowledge that demands trusting relationships with the people the researcher observes *in situ* for long periods of time. That is why ethnography was advantageous in examining GAP, where the focus was on the experiences and voices of residents that emerged from observation, dialogue and collaborations with the researcher.

## References

Agier, M., (2011) *Antropologia da cidade: Lugares, situações, movimentos [Anthropology of the city: Places, situations, movements]*, São Paulo: Terceiro Nome.

Arantes, O., (2000) Uma estratégia fatal: A cultura nas novas gestões urbanas [A fatal strategy: Culture in the new urban managements], in Arantes, O., Rainer, C. and Maricato, E., (eds.) *A cidade do pensamento único: desmanchando consensos [The city of unique thinking: breaking consensus]*, Petrópolis: Vozes.

Borges, L., (2016) *O bairro onde ninguém quer entrar já 'recebe mais visitas que os museus' [The area no-one wants to go into now has 'more visitors than museums]*, *Público*, 12 May.

Burgess, R., (1997) *A pesquisa de terreno: Uma introdução [In the Field: an introduction to field research]*, Oeiras: Celta.

Campo, R., (2010) *Porque pintamos a cidade? Uma abordagem etnográfica do graffiti urbano [*Why do we paint the city? An ethnographic approach to urban graffiti*]*, Lisboa: Fim de Século.

de Certeau, M., (2011) *A invenção do cotidiano: 'Artes de fazer' [The practice of everyday life: 'Arts of making']*, Petrópolis: Vozes

Diário de Notícas (DN)., (2014) *Arte Urbana para recuperar imagem da Quinta do Mocho [Urban Art to recover Quinta do Mocho's image]*, 3 October.

Ferro, L., (2016) *Da rua para o mundo: Etnografia urbana comparada do graffiti e do parkour [*From the *street to the world*: Comparative urban ethnography of graffiti and parkour*]*, Lisboa: ICS.

Geertz, C., (2008) *A interpretação das culturas [The interpretation of cultures]*, Rio de Janeiro: LTC.

Holston, J., (2013) *Cidadania insurgente: Disjunções da democracia e da modernidade no Brasil [Insurgent citizenship: Disjunctions of democracy and modernity in Brazil]*, São Paulo: Companhia das Letras.

Lefebvre, H. (2012), *O direito à cidade [Right to the City]*, Lisboa: Estúdio e Livraria Letra Livre.

Magnani, J. G., (2002) De perto e de dentro: Notas para uma etnografia urbana [From close up and within: Notes for an urban ethnography], *Revista Brasileira de Ciências Sociais*, 17(49):11-29.

Magnani, J. G., (2009) Etnografia urbana [Urban ethnography], in Fortuna, C. and Proença Leite, R., (eds.) *Plural de cidade: Novos léxicos urbanos [Plural of city: New urban lexicons]*, Coimbra: Edições Almedina.

Mitchell, J. C., (2009) A dança kalela: aspectos das relações sociais entre africanos urbanizados na Rodésia do Norte [The Kalela dance: aspects of social relationships among urban Africans in Northern Rhodesia], in Feldman-Bianco, B., (ed.) *Antropologia das sociedades contemporâneas: Métodos [*Anthropology of contemporary societies: Methods*]*, São Paulo: UNESP.

Shapiro, R. and Heinich, N., (2013) Quando há artificação? [When is artification?], *Sociedade e Estado*, 28(1):14-28.

Souza, R., (2008) *O discurso do protagonismo juvenil [The discourse of youth protagonism]*, São Paulo: Paulus.

Tommasi, L., (2013) Culturas de periferia: Entre o mercado, os dispositivos de gestão e o agir político [Cultures in urban peripheries: Market, management dispositives and political action], *Política & Sociedade*, 12(23):11-34.

Troillot, M-R., (2011) *Transformaciones globales: La antropología y el mundo moderno [Global transformations: Anthropology and the modern world]*, Bogotá: Universidad del Cauca e CESO / Universidad de los Andes.

TSF., (2015) *Um bairro problemático transformado em Galeria de Arte Pública* [A problematic area transformed into a Public Art Gallery], 29 October.

## Ethnography and Education publications

Titles in the series include:

*Creative learning: European experiences*, edited by Bob Jeffrey;

*Researching education policy: Ethnographic experiences*, Geoff Troman, Bob Jeffrey and Dennis Beach;

*Education and the commodity problem: Ethnographic investigations of creativity and performativity in Swedish schools*. Dennis Beach and Marianne Dovemark;

*Performing English with a postcolonial accent: Ethnographic narratives from Mexico*, Angeles Clemente and Michael J. Higgins.

*How to do Educational Ethnography*, edited by Geoffrey Walford

*Ritual and Identity; The staging and performing of rituals in the lives of young people*, Christoph Wulf et al.

*Young people's influence and democratic education: Ethnographic studies in upper secondary schools*, edited by Elisabet Öhrn, Lisbeth Lundahl and Dennis Beach

*Learner biographies and learning cultures: Identity and apprenticeship in England and Germany*, Michaela Brockmann

*Learning care lessons: Literacy, love, care and solidarity*, by Maggie Feeley

*Fair and competitive? Critical perspectives on contemporary Nordic schooling*, editors, Anne-Lise Arnesen, Elina Lahelma, Lisbeth Lundahl and Elisabet Öhrn

*Identity and social interaction in a multi-ethnic classroom*, by Ruth Barley

*The postmodern professional: Contemporary learning practices, dilemmas and perspectives*, edited by Karen Borgnakke, Marianne Dovemark and Sofia Marques da Silva

*Troubling educational cultures in the Nordic countries*, edited by Touko Vaahtera, Anna-Maija Niemi, Sirpa Lappalainenand Dennis Beach

Further information available at

www.tufnellpress.co.uk

or

www.ethnographyandeducation.org